SO YOU LOVE
TIGER STADIUM, TOO

(Give it a hug)

By Joe Falls and Irwin Cohen

Printed and bound in the United States of America.

03 02 01 00 99   5 4 3 2 1

ISBN 0-9673996-0-2

All photos courtesy of Doc Holcomb and Irwin Cohen except the following: pages 13, 54, 68, courtesy of Jim Grey, page 142 copyright status unknown.

Hall of Fame Plaques are courtesy of:
National Baseball Hall of Fame Library

Panorama of Tiger Stadium, by Bill Goff, Inc. page 38

Cartoon on page 116 courtesy of Mike Moran

Published by
Connection Graphics
Grand Ledge, Michigan

This book is dedicated to the fans who supported the Tigers
all through the 20th century.

CONTENTS OF MEMORIES

...and here it is–the place we love to go

Knowing how to read is helpful in going to Tiger Stadium

A Few Things You Might Not Know About Tiger Stadium . . .

When slugging teams came to Detroit, manager Ty Cobb had the groundskeepers put in temporary bleachers so that long drives would be just ground rule doubles.

The rightfield second deck overhangs the lower deck by 10 feet.

In the 1930s and 40s, there was a 315 marker on the second deck in rightfield.

It is just 85 feet from the front of the upper deck to home plate - or five feet less than from home plate to first base.

The Tigers claim only 2,500 seats have obstructed views due to the posts in the upper and lower decks.

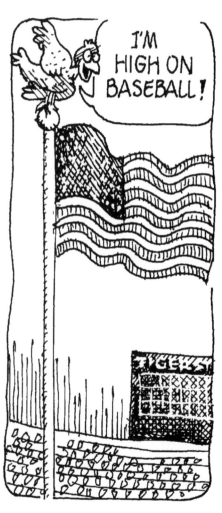

The flagpole is 125 feet high. It is the highest outfield obstacle in play in the history of baseball.

When Ty Cobb played, the groundskeepers soaked the area in front of home plate to slow down his bunts and make the ground slippery for the fielders. The area was known as "Cobb's Lake."

Jim Campbell always bragged about the size of the hot dogs in his ball park: "Six to a pound," he would proclaim with great pride. (But, lo, he never put in brown mustard.)

Question: How come nobody ever calls it "Trumbull and Michigan?"

Ty Cobb may have been a great gate attraction in his day but not on July 11, 1910 in St. Louis. He came to town with the Tigers and only 66 people showed up to watch him perform against the St. Louis Browns.

Baseball's tallest flagpole. God Bless it. See you downtown.

Jim Schmakel, *clubhouse man: "When the players come in after a bad night, they want to shout, hit the wall or throw their spikes. Jack Morris came in one night and he was furious. This was before we had our new ceiling put in. We had orange wires twisted all over the place up there.*

We had this garbage can blocking his way, so he kicked it. It was a good field goal. It went up into the air, circling like a football, end over end. The garbage can was full and it went sailing over those orange wires. It landed perfectly, and none of the garbage spilled. He wanted to make a mess and he kicked a perfect three-pointer.

Where else do they hug stadiums? We've done it in Detroit - not once, but twice. The fans couldn't help themselves. They circled the stadium, held hands, and gave it two big smooches. We love the old place, too.

By Joe Falls

The thing I will miss most about Tiger Stadium are all the empty seats.

Not on game day. But when the game is over.

How many days, how many nights, did I sit in the press box when the game was over and our work was done and look out at the empty stadium. The ushers and guards had gone home and the groundscrew was finished with their work and all that remained were those empty seats. Those lovely empty seats.

So peaceful.

So quiet.

So serene.

When the game is on, you must share the Grand Lady with others. They may love her, too. But later, when the show is over and the lights are dimmed, it is just the two of us, sharing a precious moment or two, and there is a strange feeling of warmth, as if she understands me and I understand her.

Some nights, when the corridors are empty and I am walking out of the ball park, I will turn into one of the exits and sit in one of the empty seats and take in the whole majestic scene.

The lights may be out but it doesn't matter. I can still see her and touch her and the most remarkable thing of all is that I am not thinking anything, just floating along in a strange sort of reverie.

My mind is at rest. I'd asked it to work for the past few hours and now it is time to enjoy the still of the night.

No need to think.

No need to talk.

No need even to listen.

Sit back. Relax. Reflect on what is good about our world, since our world seems so far away.

What could happen in a quiet, empty ballpark?

Truth is, I did this a lot as the 1999 season was winding down. I chose to hold her hand as much as possible.

For years I would find myself gazing out to the upper deck in right. If there was any part of this ballpark which I liked the most, it was the upper deck in right.

Not so much the overhang, which everyone talks about, but those neat rows of seats and the way they embraced the balls hit up there.

I always felt the balls hit into the upper deck in right were so much more elegant than those hit to left. You have to pound the ball to get it upstairs in left, but in right, you can kind of loft it into the seats, gently, surely, with a touch of grace. The ball rises in the air, hangs for a moment and then settles softly into the seats.

I sat next to Tom Gage, our baseball writer at The Detroit News, in the press box, and I caught him looking around at the old place, trying to drink it all in. He, too, is a bit of a hambone. I asked him one day what he thought of Tiger Stadium and without hesitation, he said:

"I love Tiger Stadium."

Tom has covered the Tigers for our newspaper for the past 21 years. Few have done it longer in the American League. Just one, I think. Some guy out in Oakland.

He sat in the same spot for all 21 years and I asked him if he planned to take his seat with him.

"No," he said. "But I plan to take a lot of pictures from right here so I can remember how everything looked."

I was troubled walking through the corridors under the stands and seeing how dark and dingy it was in there. I never liked the Tiger Plaza (the sliders are a poor imitation of the real thing), and it was sad not seeing the old faces in the front office - Alice Sloan, Dan Ewald,

The press box elevator, where one ancient writer has spent more than four days of his life riding up and down.

Rick Ferrell, Bill Lajoie, Joe McDonald and, of course, the Big Buddha

himself, Jim Campbell, the boss.

Truth is, I didn't go up there very much when these people were moved out, except to see John McHale, Jr., the president, who truly reminds me of his father, who ran the club in the late 1950s.

But now another game is over and it is time to go. I must force myself to head for my car across the street and what fun is that because all that is out there is a thing called reality. That's no fun at all.

Joe Falls holds up the no parking sign, which proves he is good for something.

By Irwin Cohen

My least favorite Tiger Stadium memory took place on a gorgeous late August day in 1992. It happened on the executive floor of the front office building. I was fired. Terminated. I didn't make the transition from the Monaghan pizza regime to the Ilitch one.

I was hired in 1983 as Director of Group Ticket Sales but was history in 1992.

Our employees were told to gather at 5 p.m. in the front lobby outside of the elevator on the third floor for a meeting. I was looking forward to it and came armed with pages of ideas, including a plan to turn Michigan Avenue into a sort of Hollywood Boulevard by having Tiger greats plant impressions of their hands and feet and their autographs into cement.

Enter here, all ye mortals who wish to build a champion.

We all milled around in this small alcove with its light green painted walls and four old wooden chairs, which were occupied with some of the veteran employees - ones who had been there for years and years. They stared silently at the blue carpeted floor.

"This looks more like a waiting room of a dentist's office," I said to my quiet co-workers.

We were told we would be called, one by one, down the hall by the back elevator. One of the ladies who had arrived on the scene before our group informed us that she looked down the hall and saw one of the girls from the accounting department. "She came out of the room crying and went down the back elevator," she said.

I still wasn't worried and figured I'd be working for the new owner the following day. One thing was clear, though. This wasn't the meeting we were told to expect. Every 10 minutes, two of us were called to the two last rooms down the hall. Our co-workers didn't return and inform us of what had transpired. We just heard the back elevator door opening and closing.

When it was my turn, the man in the room - a lawyer, I presumed, said: "Sit down, Irwin." He informed me I was not being offered employment under the new ownership. He spoke of severance pay and temporary health care but while I was looking directly at him, I wasn't listening.

I was in a mild state of shock.

The security guard told me: "They want you to clean out your desk now." He seemed quite sad.

It was after six o'clock and I told him I'd like to come back tomorrow to do it. That way I could take another look at the ball park. "Sure," he said, "but don't tell anyone I agreed or I'll be history, too."

My car sported Tiger decals on the front and rear bumpers. I scraped them off before I got into the front seat. How could I care for an organization that didn't want me?

I returned the next day and cleaned out. I didn't rush it. Instead of two arms full, I took a bit at a time stretching out the only job I had at the time.

"I'd like to take a last look at the stadium before I leave," I told the guard. He okayed my request with the instructions that I slipped past him while he was parking a player's car, if anyone asked.

I entered the stadium near the visitor's clubhouse and walked slowly through the corridor and sat near the Tigers' bullpen. I made my way back to the dugout and sat down even with third base.

The memories started to run. I stared at the leftfield stands and recalled coming to my first game over 40 years earlier. I was a little day camper and it was the summer of '49. It rained and they never played.

I even thought of the big, brown desk I was given in the

Say "Hi" to the Tigers of 2012

front office. It reeked of history. The desk belonged to Frank Navin, the longtime owner of the team, and I thought of all the decisions he made from behind that desk.

My favorite memory of Tiger Stadium? It happened early in the 1999 season. I took my grandson to a game on his fifth birthday and his eyes were as wide as mine when I saw my first game. I can't remember anything about the game in '99 but little Yudi is still talking about his day of wonder.

And that's what it is all about.

Tough old bird, Ty Cobb. He never talked about being a diabetic in his playing days in Detroit

One of the great feats in the history of Tiger Stadium was Tom Dowd, traveling secretary of the Boston Red Sox, eating 18 double scoops of ice cream in the press box during a doubleheader - a dish an inning.

Sign on the door to the visitor's clubhouse: "Visitor's Dressing Room - No Visitors Allowed."

Rocky Colavito was the first player to throw a ball out of Tiger Stadium. The fans got on him when he made an awkward catch in leftfield and he got so mad he threw the ball over the roof down the rightfield line.

The Rock was worshipped in Cleveland but got less than royal treatment in Detroit. One writer wrote: "The Tigers are putting him in left field since he has the feet for it."

And, lo, the same writer infuriated Colavito by keeping count of his RNBI's - runs NOT batted in.

The smallest crowd was 404 for a game against Boston on Sept. 24, 1928. They sold only 24 hot dogs that day. Please don't look it up.

In the days of Ty Cobb, it was a tradition on Labor Day for the men in the stands to sail their derbies onto the field the first time the Tigers did anything positive. It was their way of signifying the end of summer. Cobb would have the groundskeepers pick up all the hats and take them back to his farm in Georgia and put them on the heads of his donkeys to keep them out of the hot sun.

Father Vincent Joseph Horken, retired Catholic priest: The swells from the Detroit Athletic Club would have the best seats in the house, right near the Tiger dugout,

but they didn't sit in them. They liked to sit in the centerfield bleachers so they could rag Ty Cobb.

They would get on him, yelling all sorts of things, and you could see Cobb fuming. He never turned around to look at them. He would go to home plate, smack a triple and steal home, and when he would come back out to centerfield he would say: "Take that you so-and-so's."

Cobb also picked up all the slivers of soap on the floor of the shower room and took those back to Georgia, too.

If you've wondered if the measurements down the foul lines were accurate - 325 to right and 340 to left - don't worry. They are accurate. We measured them.

May 2, 1939 was a significant date in Tiger Stadium. It was the day Lou Gehrig's streak of 2,130 consecutive games came to an end - and the day Gates Brown was born.

Infielder-pitcher, Joe Yeager wore no glove for the Tigers in 1901-1903.

In the old days, not all teams played on Sundays, and some dressed at their hotel before heading out to the ball park. Harry Heilmann was sitting in his hotel lobby one Sunday morning when a minister came by and admonished him for playing on Sunday.

"Well, you do your work on Sunday," said Heilmann.

"Yes," replied the minister, "but I'm in the right field."

"So am I, " replied Heilmann, "and ain't that sun hell!"

Al Benton, who pitched for the Tigers in the 30s and 40s, was the only pitcher to face both Babe Ruth and Mickey Mantle.

A Tribute to Hank Greenberg

By Edgar Guest, Sr.
(1934)

58 HOME RUNS —IN 1938

Now the Irish didn't like it
When they heard of Greenberg's fame
For they thought a good first baseman
Should possess an Irish name;

And the Murphys and Mulrooneys
Said they never dreamed they'd see
A Jewish boy from Bronxville
Out where Casey used to be.

And in the early days of April
Not a Dugan tipped his hat
Or prayed to see a "double"
When Hank Greenberg came to bat.

In July the Irish wondered
Where he ever learned to play.
He makes me think of Casey
Old Man Murphy dared to say;

And with 57 doubles
And a score of homers made
The respect they had for Greenberg
was being openly displayed.

But on the Jewish New Year
When Hank Greenberg came to bat
And made two home runs off pitcher Rhodes–
they cheered like mad for that

Came Yom Kippur, holy fast day
Worldwide over to the Jew–
And Hank Greenberg to his teaching
And the old tradition true

Spent the day among his people
and he didn't come to play.
Said Murphy to Mulrooney
"We shall lose the game today!

We shall miss him on the infield
And shall miss him at the bat,
But he's true to his religion–
And I honor him for that!"

QUIRKY MANAGERS

George Stallings (1901): He put his players in black and brown stockings because the fans would think they were "tiger stripes."

Frank Dwyer (1902): A former player and umpire, he took over with high hopes but left talking to himself when his team compiled the worst batting average in the league and his best pitcher, Ed Siever, won eight games. Result: 30 1/2 games out and a ticket back home.

Ed Barrow (1903-04): When he was fired, he sold his $2,500 stock in the ball club for $1,400.

*****Bobby Lowe (1904):** He once hit four homers in a game, but not for the Tigers.

Bill Armour (1905-06): A nervous type, he would stop a game if he saw a butterfly on the field and make his players catch it.

Hughie Jennings (1907-20): He was considered a brainy manager but not because of a stunt while attending Cornell University. He dove in the school's swimming pool at dusk one night when there was no water in the pool.

Ty Cobb (1921-26): He astounded his players in spring training by calling off a morning workout, telling them: "Boys, sleep until noon." They still didn't like him, or trust him.

George Moriarity (1927-28): As his days were running out, he looked around at the ball park and saw the smallest crowd in Detroit history - just 404 fans. "Not enough for a game of pinochle," he grumped.

Bucky Harris (1929-33): His teams were so poor that he wanted to win something. He told one of his coaches: "Take a dozen balls home tonight and bake them in the oven. It'll make them lighter and at least we'll win the fungo hitting contest tomorrow."

Del Baker (1933): Could steal a pitcher's pitches but his players didn't believe him and paid little attention to him.

Mickey Cochrane (1934-38): He was so hyper during the 1934 World Series against the St. Louis Cardinals, he slept in a hospital instead of his own bed at home.

Steve O'Neill (1943-48): His players and coaches tried to hold him back but he once took the lineups to home plate on opening day in more than a slight state of inebriation. He was fired while cutting the grass in the front of his home in Cleveland.

Red Rolfe (1942-52): He suffered so much from colitis that he had to sit on a pillow in the dugout.

Fred Hutchinson: A bear of a man, he would break all the lights in the tunnel back to the dressing room after losing a game - then walk all the way to his home in Grosse Pointe.

Jack Tighe (1957-58): He told the rookie outfielders at training camp in Lakeland not to run onto the runways of the nearby airport to get one of the balls, even if a teammate tells him to do so. "It just means they want your job."

Bill Norman (1958-59): Drank beers two at a time after a game and uttered the same words over and over: "Some days you win, some days you lose, some days it rains."

Jimmy Dykes (1959-60): Smoked cigars all through the day, but the day he got fired he smoked a cigar but forgot to light it.

Joe Gordon (1960): He came to Detroit for Jimmy Dykes in the only trade of managers in baseball history but after looking at the Tigers for six weeks, he locked himself in his hotel room in downtown Detroit and wouldn't come out. He went back home to Oregon.

JIM BUNNING

THE FANS IN DETROIT KNOW AS MUCH ABOUT BASEBALL AS A CHINESE AVIATOR!

I KNOW HIT AND RUN.

MGR. MAYO SMITH

*Billy Hitchcock (1960): He once charged Jim Bunning with cutting the balls on his belt buckle but when he showed them to the writers, the balls looked like they were hit with an axe.

Bob Scheffing (1961-63): A bright man but when he joined Ernie Harwell in the radio booth, he began one broadcast by saying: "Good evening, everyone. This is Ernie Harwell along with Bob Scheffing . . . "

Chuck Dressen (1963-66): The dandy Little Manager spent more time in the kitchen making chili for his coaches than he did in meetings with his players.

**Bob Swift (1965-66): He hit only 13 homers in 13 years in the major leagues but could always tell you: "Yeah, but I beat the Yankees one day when I got hit with the pitch with the bases loaded in the bottom of the ninth inning."

*Frank Skaff (1966): He followed Charlie Dressen and Bob Swift, both afflicted by terminal diseases, and refused to sit in their office in the dressing room "because the last two guys went to the hospital."

Mayo Smith: (1967-70): Won a World Championship but when he was fired, he said: "The fans in Detroit know as much about baseball as Chinese aviators."

Billy Martin (1971-73): He had a dispute with one of his pitchers, Dave Boswell, and beat him up in an alley outside of the Lindell AC in downtown Detroit.

POUND THAT BUD!

MANAGER JOE SCHULTZ

*Joe Schultz: His battle cry was the same after every game: "Pound that Bud!"

Ralph Houk (1974-78): A man with a terrible temper, he would rip into people at night, and then, the next day, he would greet them with: "How are you this morning. Nice day, isn't it?"

Les Moss (1979): The poor guy lasted only six weeks and was so confused he let the fans on the field on the first day of spring training and his players couldn't even play catch.

*Dick Tracewski (1979) He never liked the limelight. When he became an interim manager, he knew he would be asked a lot of crazy questions. One time a writer asked him: "What's your favorite color?" Tracewski replied: "Geez, I thought you were going to ask me if I slept naked."

Sparky Anderson: He could not make out his lineup in his hotel room unless the TV set was on.

Buddy Bell (1996-98): He had this little habit - he liked the clubhouse man to put a beer and cigarette in an out-of-the-way place in the clubhouse because he didn't want to smoke or drink in front of his roommates.

Larry Parrish (1998-?): Hates to fly. Tries to read or play cards to take his mind off the airplane. He says, "I wish I was John Madden and could ride around the country in a bus."

(The list does not include Win Mercer. He was named manager for the 1902 season but committed suicide in San Francisco in January. He was 28 and died of inhaling poisonous fumes. He left a note warning against the evils of chasing women and gambling.)

* Interim manager

WELCOME

Ernie Harwell, broadcaster: One of the craziest things happened in the late 1970s, It was raining before the game started and Hal Middlesworth, the publicity director, called from the press box and said: "It looks like this game is going to be postponed. If it is, we'll have a doubleheader tomorrow night but don't announce it until you hear it over the intercom in about 30 minutes."

So this is where Ernie Harwell's voice comes from.

In about 30 minutes, we heard this voice over the intercom that came from the press box that said: "Game called, doubleheader Saturday."

I put this on the air and my wife Lulu, who was at the game, got into the car and started out on the expressway. We tuned in the scoreboard show with Ray Lane. He's giving the scores and all of a sudden he says: "Wait a minute, folks! That report Ernie gave was erroneous. Ernie., Ernie, wherever you are, come back!"

So we came back and they started the game and the Tigers eventually won it. I think Tony Taylor hit a double in the eighth inning.

But Jim Campbell, the general manager, was really peeved because a lot of people had radios in the ball park and they left for Battle Creek or Saginaw and they demanded their money back.

Another crazy thing happened when George Kell and I were working together. We had a mayor from one of the outstate cities come to the booth to give us this big, big wheel of cheese. To get to us, you had to come down through a hatch like getting into a submarine and he had a little too much to drink that night. He slipped coming down and dropped the wheel of cheese. It must have weighed 50 or 100 pounds.

It rolled out of the booth and fell down into the seats. This kid, maybe 8, was sitting there and it just missed him. If it had hit him, it could have killed him. The cheese splattered all over the seats and the guy never made it into our booth. In fact, we never saw him again.

When they took out the green seats at Tiger Stadium, each member of the media was given two of them as a remembrance of the old park.

Ernie Harwell placed his two on his front porch. His wife knew how much Ernie cherished these seats and the first time he went on the road with the team, she painted them black to preserve them for him.

Attention Please! There will be no school tomorrow for all Tiger fans!

It rained one Saturday and Sparky Anderson had the whole day off. He said: "They showed 13 college basketball games - from noon until 1 a.m. If you had one beer for each game, you'd be plastered."

Tiger Stadium South - sometimes known as Marchant Stadium, spring training home of the Tigers - was named after Joker Marchant, a man who worked for the recreation department in Lakeland.

Nobody is sure where he is buried but umpires better go easy when they dust off home plate.

Ernie Harwell is a devout Christian. If you go to dinner with him, everyone joins hands while he says grace.

A writer's wife showed up in spring training with four suitcases, a bag, a trunk and a cardboard box - enough gear to outfit the Russian army at Stalingrad.

She explained: "The four suitcases have clothes in them, the bag is for my cosmetics, the trunk is for cooking and the cardboard box . . . well, that's stuff we don't need."

It cost owner John Fetzer $20,000 to change the name of the ballpark from Briggs Stadium to Tiger Stadium. It would have been more but he saved a lot of money on the big sign over the ballpark, needing only a "T" and "e" from Briggs Stadium to spell out Tiger Stadium.

Alice Sloan, former executive secretary of the Tigers, worked for George Trautman, Billy Evans, Spike Briggs, John McHale, Muddy Ruel, Charlie Gehringer, Bill Dewitt, Rick Ferrell, Jim Campbell and Bo Schembechler.

They once asked outfielder Davy Jones of the Tigers the secret of his success.

He said: "I don't have a secret. I just have a Limburger sandwich and two bottles of beer before I go to bed."

Owner Frank Navin, on night baseball: "It is the beginning of the end of baseball."

Boots Poffenberger, the zany pitcher of the 1930, always woke up to the "Breakfast of Champions" - two fried eggs and a cold bottle of beer.

And, then, of course, there was catcher J.W. Porter, who would walk into coffee shops - after the games - and order: "Twenty-four, over light, please."

Ty Tyson broadcast the Tigers' first game on the radio in 1927. He was also the public address announcer and so you could hear his voice twice over the radio.

Wise old codger, Bucky Harris, he managed the Tigers for the second time in 1955-56. When he didn't want to answer a reporter's question, he would simply let out a whistle, as if to say: "That's a terrific question." Nobody ever knew how to quote his whistle.

Most famous inning in Detroit baseball history (Oct. 7, 1935):
Clifton struck out. Cochrane singled off Herman's glove. Gehringer grounded to Cavaretta, Cochrane taking second. Goslin singled to right-center, scoring Cochrane with the winning run.

In the first American League game in Detroit, Morris George (Doc) Amole of Buffalo threw a no-hitter against the Tigers. It happened in 1900 but don't look it up. The American League didn't gain major league status until 1901.

Joe Gordon, the skipper in 1960, claimed his big claim to fame is that he played his entire career without using an athletic supporter.

When Mel Ott, the National League home run champion, broadcast the Tiger games with Van Patrick in 1956-58, he was so nervous he could not light his cigarette in the broadcast booth. His hands were shaking too much.

George Cantor, *Detroit News columnist: Why is Tiger Stadium so important to the people in Detroit but all over Michigan? I think it speaks to three things. It speaks to the lost city. The Detroit that used to be, the city most people like to remember, and hope that someday will be there again. It speaks to childhood. One of the fondest memories growing up as a kid is going to the ball park. And it speaks to family because usually the first person you shared that experience with was your dad or your mother or an older brother or somebody who was very dear to you growing up.*

I can remember my first game vividly. It was against the Yankees in 1948, Joe DiMaggio hit a home run off Hal Newhouser. I can still see the ball going over the 365 sign. I didn't know who Joe DiMaggio was; I didn't know who Hal Newhouser was. They were just names, but that image is as clear as a bell. I treasure it because now I know who those guys were, and I saw this moment.

It's a special memory, just as I hope my daughter will remember the first time we went to the ball park together in 1983. She saw Lou Whitaker hit a home run and I'm sure that's something that will remain with her because that day she learned how to yell "Looooooou."

My grandfather saw Ty Cobb play and my father saw Greenberg and Gehringer and I saw Kaline and Lolich and my daughter saw Trammell and Whitaker in that ball park and that's part of all our memories and always will be.

Tough Manager.

Hughie Jennings once ordered Claude Rossman to lay down a bunt, but when Rossman crossed him up and hit a home run, Jennings fined him $50.

Poor Bill Armour, the manager in 1905-06. His wife was so caught up in the game, he had to go to her box and ask which pitchers to use.

Shortstop Ray Oyler, a member of the 1968 champions, was such a poor hitter that with two out in an inning, second baseman Dick McAuliffe, next to hit, went into the on-deck circle with his glove instead of his bat.

Oyler went 0-for-August in 1968. He also went 0-for-September.

L'AFFAIR JIM BUNNING

The Tigers were playing a night game in Baltimore and Jim Bunning was on the mound. Billy Hitchcock, manager of the Orioles, was very disturbed and kept complaining to the umpires and pointing to Bunning on the mound.

Hitchcock was livid after the game.

He complained that Bunning had been cutting the balls on his belt buckle and he had five or six of them on his desk. They looked like they had been struck with an axe, not shaved with a belt buckle.

It made a fascinating story since Bunning denied everything.

The next day, Bill Tanton, a sports writer for The Baltimore Sun, came by the Tigers' hotel lobby, where Joe Falls of *The Free Press* was sitting with Sam Greene of The News. He asked both

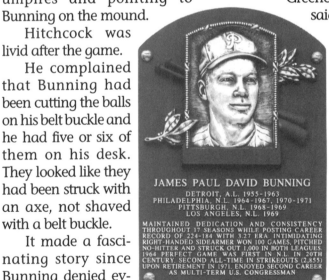

JAMES PAUL DAVID BUNNING
DETROIT, A.L. 1955-1963
PHILADELPHIA, N.L. 1964-1967, 1970-1971
PITTSBURGH, N.L. 1968-1969
LOS ANGELES, N.L. 1969

MAINTAINED DEDICATION AND CONSISTENCY THROUGHOUT 17 SEASONS WHILE POSTING CAREER RECORD OF 224-184 WITH 3.27 ERA. INTIMIDATING RIGHT-HANDED SIDEARMER WON 100 GAMES, PITCHED NO-HITTER AND STRUCK OUT 1,000 IN BOTH LEAGUES. 1964 PERFECT GAME WAS FIRST IN N.L. IN 20TH CENTURY. SECOND ALL-TIME IN STRIKEOUTS (2,855) UPON RETIREMENT IN 1971. ENJOYED SECOND CAREER AS MULTI-TERM U.S. CONGRESSMAN

men if they thought Bunning was cutting the balls.

Falls said: "I don't think so. They were chopped up so bad I don't see how he could have done it."

Greene (biting on his cigar) said: "I think he did it . . . and Hitchcock probably taught him how to do it when he was a coach in Detroit."

The stogie hid the smile on old Sam's face.

Tanton went back to his office and wrote a column about what the two writers from Detroit had to say about the controversy. He did not identify which writer said what and when Bunning saw the quotes in the paper the next day, he assumed Falls had attacked him and did not talk to him for the next two years.

HARVEY KUENN AFTER DARK

It was almost midnight in midtown Manhattan. Harvey Kuenn, who liked to tip a few, was seen lurching from the door of a bar on Lexington Avenue.

He was headed for a taxi parked at the curb, but as he reached the handle on the back door, the cab pulled away and sent him spinning around on the sidewalk. He headed straight back into the bar.

Uh, oh. The Tigers had a Sunday doubleheader with the Yankees the next day.

The Tigers won both games as Al Kaline and Kuenn got 15 hits between them.

Paul Carey, former broadcaster: The original booth hung down from the bottom of the upper deck. You had to climb through a trap door and go down a steep ladder to get into the hanger. Then you had to go along the photographer's loft to the far end next to the screen.

Howard Stitzel was our engineer in those days. Howard didn't like baseball. But he liked the surroundings. He liked the hot dogs, he liked the popcorn, he liked the food. He liked looking at the girls. He would close up his shutter and not even look at the game. He couldn't see a thing except what he wanted to see and loved every minute of it.

Paul Carey and Ernie Harwell: two stand up guys.

GREAT MOMENTS

Here are Joe Falls' 10 most memorable games in Tiger Stadium:

1. The night the Tigers won the pennant in 1968.

This was the wildest moment of all.

The place was packed with fans awaiting the magic moment. It had been so bad the year before - the year of the riots, when grief was piled atop grief as the Tigers lost out in the final inning of the final game. In fact, it went down to the final batter, with Dick McAuliffe hitting into a double play - his only one of the season.

Now, the Tigers went down to the final inning again. They were playing the Yankees and they batted in the ninth inning with the score tied. They needed a victory or a Baltimore defeat in Boston.

Actually, it was all over because the Orioles lost, 2-0. Jim Campbell, the general manager, wouldn't let them put the score up because he feared the fans would rush on the field and his game would be lost by forfeit.

I kept shouting: "Put up the score! Put up the score!" I was wrong. Of course. The whole thing would have been a mess.

The Tigers pulled it out on Don Wert's single to right that scored Al Kaline from third, and the fans went wild. They climbed the outfield fences and rushed onto the field. It was a mad scene, with fireworks going off and everyone screaming and running around in circles.

I was looking around for our guys who were covering the game with me, but they were gone. They were headed downstairs for the clubhouse celebration. None of us had ever seen a pennant-clinching game and they wanted to be in on the fun.

I was left alone, at deadline.

So, I started writing two stories at once - my column and a story of the game. One take of the column, one take of the game story, and so on. I was pretty confused but it worked out OK. We made the edition.

It was all worth it because when all our writing was done, we went over to the State Bar to celebrate, papering the walls with all the replates of our paper as each new edition came out. We went on until 5 a.m. and it was great to see all the guys so happy.

2. Mickey Mantle's over-the-roof shot in 1956

None of us had seen anything like this, either, and I can still see the ball rising toward the rightfield roof, taking one hop, and disappearing into Trumbull Ave.

Ted Williams had hit one out in 1939. But now it was 17 years later before anyone else could do it.

The day after Mantle connected, we got the idea of setting up a "Mantle Shift" in our paper, The Detroit Times. We had Kaline pose in a fielding position, with his hands on his knees, then took a picture of the rightfield roof where Mantle's shot went out.

We had our artist at the paper reduce Kaline's picture and paste it to the rightfield roof. It looked terrific.

When John McHale, Sr., general manager of the Tigers, came to work in the morning, he saw the picture and, with great alarm, called the managing editor of The Times, John Manning. McHale complained bitterly about us putting his best player on the edge of the roof. Manning didn't know what to say to him. The picture looked legitimate to him.

When Mr. Manning found out we were just having some fun, he called McHale and explained it all to him. "OK," said McHale, "but don't take him up there again."

3. Ozzie Virgil's first game in Tiger Stadium in 1938

He was the Tigers' first black player and he broke in with a bang at home - going 5-for-5.

It so happened manager Bill Norman was down on me for some of the things I had written about him and he wouldn't let anyone into the dressing room - especially me - to talk to Virgil. All the reporters, broadcasters and photographers were shut out.

Virgil left through the tunnel to the Tigers' dugout and went out into the night without saying a word to anyone.

Everyone wondered what was going on. I said: "Search me. I have no idea."

4. Denny McLain's 30th victory in 1968

A mad day in Detroit. The maestro was on the verge of creating history and it seemed half the country showed up for the event.

Dizzy Dean, the last pitcher to win 30 games, was on hand, but was thrown out of the press box by Watson Spoelstra, chairman of the Detroit Baseball Writers' Association, because Dean wasn't a member of the press.

The Tigers pulled it out for Denny in the bottom of the ninth and, as the fans swarmed on the field, Denny spent the next half hour or so walking around the field accepting the plaudits of everyone.

When he was asked how he planned to celebrate the moment, he said: "I'll be with my wife. We'll think of something."

5. Joe, the Peacemaker

In Chicago, Tiger outfielder Al Cowens charged the mound toward White Sox pitcher Ed Farmer in retaliation for being hit the previous season. A battle royal nearly ensued. There was bad blood on both sides and it looked like there would be an eruption when the White Sox came to Detroit a few days later.

The newspapers played it up big.

Some fans turned out for the expected fisticuffs and I didn't like it. I went into the Chicago dressing room and asked Farmer what he would do it Cowens offered him his hand.

He said: "I'd take it."

I hustled down to the Detroit dressing room and asked Cowens the same question and got the same answer.

So, while almost no one was looking, Farmer and Cowens took the starting lineups to home plate and shook hands. OK, I felt good about it.

6. Gibby's Home Run

None of us will ever forget Kirk Gibson's wild war dance around the bases after he wrapped up the 1984 World Series with a three-run homer off Goose Gossage in the eighth inning.

But I had other things on my mind. I could see those people gathering in the streets outside the stadium, ready to let loose if the Tigers won the game. I could hear the drums beating and it was very scary.

And we all know what happened - another black eye for Detroit as they rioted in the streets, burning a police car and killing a man when he came out of one of the Coney Island restaurants in downtown Detroit.

7. Rumble, Rumble

Two earthquakes shook the ball park a few years apart. They came from other Midwestern states and while the players couldn't feel it on the field, the press box swayed each time.

The second time I went into the back room and leaned on the lunch counter and pretended it wasn't happening. But it was, and it was scary. Nothing like San Francisco but very unsettling anyway.

8. Harmon Killebrew's shot over the leftfield roof.

This occurred on a Friday night in 1962. It came off Jim Bunning. The Minnesota slugger was the first one to put a ball over the leftfield roof. He sent the ball high down the line and it took two bounces on the roof and disappeared.

What made it so strange is that I was fooling around with Tony Adamkic. The Associated Press teletype operator. I gave him a fake sing-song call as Killebrew came to the plate: "Harmon Killebrew became the first man in history to put the ball over the leftfield roof . . . "

When the ball went out, Tony chased me around the press box and kept punching me in the arm, saying: "Nobody can call that one - nobody!"

The next day, Killebew said five people called him at his downtown hotel and offered him the ball.

9. Seven-Hour Game

I was the official scorer when the Tigers and Yankees went seven hours in a 22-inning game in 1961. It was my job to give the official time.

I looked at the clock on the centerfield scoreboard and could not tell if it was closer to 8:29 or 8:30. I waited for a moment before picking up the press box microphone, knowing a seven-hour game would be more historic than one that went 6:59.

So, I said: "Time of game - seven hours." I wasn't sure but all the guys in the press box cheered. Except Jerry Green, my colleague at The News. I don't think he wanted me to be a part of such an historic moment and told people for years that the real time was 6:59. And darned if I didn't recently read a story of the game where the lady writer called it six hours and 59 minutes.

10. Don't Knock the Rock

It was a lazy day in the ball park. Not much was happening. Rocky Colavito, my antagonist on the Tigers, came up and lifted a soft fly to rightfield. An easy play.

Sam Bowens, the Baltimore rightfielder, came charging in and ran right under the ball. It landed 10 feet behind him.

I was the official scorer and Jerry Green, who was sitting next to me, said: "That ball has to be caught. Can you call it an error?"

Why not?

I picked up the press box microphone and said: "Error 9."

Then I made the mistake of my life. I went into the Detroit dressing room and as I was talking to manager Charlie Dressen, Colavito burst into the room and picked me up out of my chair and held me against the wall.

He was holding me by the throat and screaming at me. The screaming I didn't mind. I'd been screamed at before. I didn't like his choke hold. My feet were six inches off the floor. Dressen pulled Colavito away and said: "You can't kill the guy."

That's right. But he gave it a good try.

Virgil Trucks: *It was 1952 and not many people were in the park. Most of them were downtown watching a parade for Gen. Douglas McArthur.*

It was a crazy day. I had a no-hitter going and it was the bottom of the ninth and the game was scoreless. Bob Porterfield was pitching for Washington and he was pitching a great game. We got our first hit off him in the seventh inning - a double by Vic Wertz - but he got picked off at second. So, it was 0-0 and I wondered if I was going to get my no-hitter or would I have to go out there and pitch some more.

Wertz came up with two out in the ninth and knocks the ball into the upper deck for a home run and I have my no-hitter. I want to be the first one out there to greet him at home plate but when I jumped up I hit my head on the dugout roof and almost knocked myself out.

Clubhouse Comedy:

Joe Sparma played quarterback for the Ohio State football team before he became a pitcher for the Tigers.

He was sitting in front of his locker in Tiger Stadium and told a writer that he'd like to play football again.

"How much do you think I could get for playing with the Detroit Lions?" he asked.

"About $50,000," replied the writer.

"That much?" said Sparma

"Sure," said the writer. "The Tigers would give you that much to play football again."

Pitcher Dave Wickersham - circa 1960s - was asked if he ever hit a home run.

"No," he said, "but I once hit the wall on 50 bounces."

Ed Browalski of the Polish Daily News covered the Tigers and had a keen sense of humor.

He said: "I just found out that Polish American Night is going to be on Sept. 4 this year. The Tigers will be in Oakland."

Mickey Lolich was a very composed pitcher. One night the wind was blowing furiously in Tiger Stadium.

He was asked: "Does the wind ever bother you?"

"Naw," he said. "When it blows to right, I just lean left."

Statistic: When Jim Northrup played quarterback at Alma College in 1959, he led the nation's small colleges in passing and total yardage.

Signs of the times. . .past

Hal Naragon, a coach with the 1968 champions, was asked for his biggest thrill in the majors.

"It was the day I knocked in the winning run in a big game for Cleveland," he said. "It came with two out in the bottom of the ninth."

"Tell me about it."

"I walked with the bases loaded."

When the Tigers had a minor league team at Jamestown, N.Y., they would have one lady selling tickets at the ticket booth and two men taking the tickets at the gate.

Isn't that a slight imbalance?

"Naw," said one of the ticket takers. "Somebody has to chase the foul balls hit into the street."

El Goof-oh:

Guess which reporter - who shall go nameless - wrote a front-page for The Detroit Times naming Bill Rigney the new manager of the Tigers in 1961?

One week later the Tigers hired Bob Scheffing.

Two weeks later the Detroit Times went out of business.

Why these Tigers liked to play:

Jack Morris: "I like embarrassing players on other teams. I like making them look bad . . . because that's what they're trying to do to me."

Enos Cabell: "I like jumping around and getting dirty."

Milt Wilcox: "I don't know why I like it. I never think about being a ball player."

Alan Trammell: "Being a baseball player means I don't have to go into the real world."

The big moment arrived: Denny McLain meeting Bob Gibson at the start of the 1968 World Series. Microphones were being pinned to their uniforms for a pre-game interview.

The world wondered what the two best pitchers in baseball would have to say when they met for the first time.

"You go first, Denny" the producer said to McLain.

McLain said: "One, two, three, four."

Gibson replied: "Five, six, seven eight."

The Twins were playing the Tigers in Tiger Stadium when the press box phone rang.

The voice said: "Get Boswell up."

"This is the press box. Who do you want?"

"I said I want Dave Boswell."

"Then you'd better call the bullpen."

Willie Horton, *former outfielder: As a kid growing up in Detroit, I used to slip in the back gate. One day me and my buddy got caught and they took us around to the front office. I thought we were going to get it but they let us go.*

We used to go to the ball park after school. We'd wait until the big truck would pull up delivering stuff to the ball park. We'd go in behind them and wind up with the best seats in the house.

I guess the greatest thing that happened as a player was the day we threw out Lou Brock at the plate in the 1968 World Series. People say that's what turned it around for us. I think about that play every time I go to the ball park.

We used to talk every day, us outfielders, how we would make different plays. I mean, Al Kaline, Jim Northrup, Mickey Stanley and myself. We didn't have TV tape in those days but we would look at the movie films. We noticed a few things about Brock. When he went around second on a hit to the outfield, he'd kind of drift into third base. He did the same thing going home from second base. He'd slow up a little. We noticed that the third base coach was relaxed because that was Lou Brock running, and the next batter at the plate didn't give him any help coming home.

So, when the ball came to me, I figured we had a chance to get him and I let it fly. Bill Freehan did a great job of blocking the plate and we were still in the game and the Series.

They used to serve hard drinks in the press box (circa 1950s) and one day a foul ball came sailing back and smashed into the glass where Lloyd Northard of the UPI was sitting. It cut the glass in half in a perfectly smooth pattern and didn't spill a drop of the drink.

Maury Hendry, the Western Union telegrapher, used to take a lot of kidding from the writers in the press box as he scrambled after foul balls which came up to the third deck.

"Go get 'em, Maury!" they would cry out. It was strange sight, at that, to see such an old geezer chasing down the bounding balls.

The laughter stopped when the writers found out that Maury was collecting the balls for the young boys at the Starr Commonwealth home in outstate Michigan. In fact, they started tossing him the ones they caught.

When Sparky Anderson was the manager, the dugout floor would be covered with sunflower seeds at the end of the game.

That was nothing compared to Ralph Houk's slimy tobacco juice which made the floor slippery. The writers always went home with brown shoes.

Ty Cobb left a hambone nailed to a table in the clubhouse so the players could hone their bats. They used it so much, they wore it out. Or they made pea soup out of it.

Maybe the most memorable line Joe Falls ever wrote in Tiger Stadium was: "Jimmie Piersall picked the ball up in centerfield and threw it into the Cleveland dugout and hit manager Joe Adcock on the fly."

Who remembers when Mickey Lolich used to drive to the ball park on his motorcycle? That's OK. Tom Monaghan came in on his helicopter.

The first female reporter to cover a game in Detroit was Jackie Lapin, a summer intern from the Free Press in 1968. A male writer from another paper tried to throw her out but thought better of it when 12 other writers stood up to him.

Oakland relief pitcher Paul Lindblad liked to use a minesweeper to see what he could find in the grass of American League ball parks. One day he found two spent bullets in the grass at Tiger Stadium.

Dennis Archer, *mayor of Detroit: Growing up as a youngster, I was Frank Lary, the great Tiger pitcher, the Yankee Killer. We used to play ball at the side of our school building, trying to strike each other out with a tennis ball. I'd give 'em the old Frank Lary stare, then cut loose.*

DETROIT MAYOR ARCHER

How can any of us forget 1967? It was the year of the riot, the year the Tigers nearly won the pennant. They didn't do it, but came back the next year and did. That gave us all a lift - the City of Detroit, Southeastern Michigan and the entire state.

And how I remember the 1984 World Series. My wife and I were in the stands and that's when the big song was "Ghost Busters." But they would play "Goose Busters" in the ball park . . . for Goose Gossage, the great San Diego relief pitcher. And when Kirk Gibson hit the ball into the upper deck against him to win the game and clinch the World Series - it seemed like Babe Ruth standing at the plate and pointing out to rightfideld.

As long as there is a person who has been to Tiger Stadium, that stadium will never die.

SAL'S SAD STORY

H.G. Salsinger, venerable sports editor of the *Detroit News*, covered the Tigers for 50 years . . . until that fateful day in 1954.

He was writing about the opener against the Baltimore Orioles when a foul ball off the bat of Tiger pitcher Steve Gromek came flying into the crowded press box.

"Look out!" shouted Lyall Smith, sports editor of the Free Press.

Mr. Salsinger looked up from his typewriter and the ball hit him squarely in the face. It knocked him off his chair and sent him sprawling to the back wall about eight feet away.

The ball must have hit an artery because blood began spurting from his eye. It went back over where he was sitting in the second row, cleared the first row and went down to where the fans were sitting in the upper deck behind home plate.

Mr. Salsinger was in a state of shock.

He was taken by stretcher to an ambulance and rushed to the hospital. He lost the sight of his eye and never returned to the ball park.

H.G. Salsinger. A great name in the history of the Tigers.

The following celebrities have called Detroit their home and were familiar with Tiger Stadium:

Tim Allen
Sonny Bono
Alice Cooper
Francis Ford Coppola
Aretha Franklin
Julie Harris
Piper Laurie
Elmore (Dutch) Leonard
Charles Lindberg
Joe Louis
Madonna
Ed McMahon
Ted Nugent
George Peppard
Della Reese
Smokey Robinson
Dianna Ross
George C. Scott
Bob Seger
Tom Selleck
Tom Skerrit
Lily Tomlin
Robert Wagner
Robin Williams and
Stevie Wonder.

And did you know that Detroit was the first city to assign individual telephone numbers and is considered the home of the typewriters.

This is not Raphael Palmeiro in a Detroit uniform. It's the substitute first baseman, Tom Selleck.

Tony Spina was a friendly man, and a great photographer for *The Free Press*. He just didn't know a lot about the games.

One day good old Tony was shooting his pictures in front of the screen behind home plate. He was crouched low so he wouldn't block anyone's view.

The pitcher let loose with a wild pitch. The ball went back to the wall, with the catcher in pursuit. Spina, always the gentleman, picked the ball up and flipped it to the catcher.

Jim Price, *former catcher: Nobody liked to play baseball more than Norm Cash. He was a terrific person. We roomed together in 1971 and he and Billy Martin, our manager, liked to go out and have a good time. I was not fond of drinking, but I had nothing against it. I became the designated driver. I was the guy who made sure everyone got back to the hotel.*

We were in Kansas City and went to a couple of hangouts. Norm and Billy had a few drinks - probably more than a few - and it was about four or five in the morning when we got back to the hotel. I put Norm over my shoulder and carried him up through the freight elevator in the old fireman's carry.

When we got to the room, I threw him on the bed and the phone started ringing. Understand now, we're in Kansas City, the sun is coming up and Norm is out of it. This was when he wasn't married and he picked up the phone and it was one of his girlfriends. They started arguing and Norm pulled the phone out of the wall and threw it out the window. Then he took off his watch and threw that out the window.

I couldn't believe it. I knew it was a good watch and I looked out the window and there it was laying in the back alley. We had a doubleheader coming up that afternoon but I knew it was an expensive watch and I started down to get it. I took the freight elevator down and I was only wearing my skivvies.

I started picking up the pieces to the watch when I felt a tap on my shoulder. It was one of Kansas City's finest. He said: "Young man, can I help you? You look awfully good in those shorts." I thought, uh, oh, now I'm in trouble. He took me to his station house and I figured they were going to arrest me for indecent exposure. I did some fast talking, telling them who I was and what happened, and they let me go. I promised them some tickets for the afternoon doubleheader and some autographed baseballs.

I caught both games that day and went 0-for-8. Cash got six or seven hits and drove in five runs - Norman Cash, one of the greatest guys I've ever known, one of a kind.

When the press box burned down in the winter of 1977, general manager Jim Campbell stood in centerfield and told one of the fireman: "What a shame. There are no writers up there at this time of year."

What happens at the mound when a manager goes out to talk to his pitcher? Dan Petry is struggling and here comes Sparky Anderson from the dugout.

Anderson: "It must be a hundred degrees out here."

Petry: "Yep, it sure is hot."

Anderson: "You've thrown a lot of pitches. How do you feel?"

Petry: "How do you think I feel?"

Anderson: "Well, you're going to feel a lot worse, because you're leaving."

Dave Bergman remembers the first time he ever touched a baseball.

"My mom would walk my brother and I around the block, pushing a stroller for us. I'd be carrying a whiffle ball bat. I'd get out of the stroller and she'd pitch to me. I'd give the ball a whack and go get it."

Wise old guy, centerfielder Billy Bruton. He was howling with laughter the day he retired in 1964.

"Fooled you guys all the way," he told the press. "You think I'm quitting at 36. I am 40. I cheated four years on you"

The working press box. Except nobody's working. They're all watching TV.

The Fetzer Letter

The darkest day in the history of baseball in Detroit was Oct. 1, 1967. It was the year of the riot - the year Detroit burned. The Tigers were in a four-way fight for the pennant and lost in the final inning off the final game - indeed, with the final batter. The fans were so angry they all but tore up the ball park after it was all over.

Owner John Fetzer - good, gray John - watched the carnage on the field, then returned to his office. He reached for pen and paper and this is what he wrote:

Look, nobody burned it up!

A TRUE CONFESSION - BY FETZER

On this infamous evening of Oct. 1, 1967, there is no happiness in that section of Mudville near the corner of Michigan and Trumbull. The heroes have fallen and I am ill. I have been here alone for hours but a few tears cannot wash away the hurt.

As I tuned in on the waves of reflection, the brilliant lights of Tiger Stadium began to fade and I watched hundreds of fans give vent to their frustrations. They destroyed scores of stadium seats and piled the rubble on the dugouts. Still others clawed at home plate and the pitcher's mound, while a bedlam of confusion turned many more hundreds into a near mob scene with the elements of combat everywhere on the playing field.

In stony silence I thought of how desperately hard I had fought to build a winner in Detroit. It seemed that my long-sought goal was near fruition. I thought a pennant would have meant more to Detroit than all of the man-made remedies put together. I thought that 1967 would be a crowning year of glory for our city and that the world would soon forget our stormy past.

But it was not to be. All season long it seemed as if a hexing magic was following each footstep. Every kind of injury stalked the ball club. We were never able to use a full line of soldiers in the infantry. Time and again we would charge but the attack was short-lived. We just could never quite get going.

My thoughts turned to what I would say to the oracles. I knew they would surely come. They always do. But this time it was different. To be sure, they made the rounds. Everyone from the front office to the clubhouse will be in the news - that is, everyone except the guy who wanted so much to do the thing Detroit wanted most. The fellow who spent a fortune trying.

I am glad to preserve my solitude. The plain unadulterated truth is that I failed to win the pennant. Pennant winners are the only heroes and the losers, even if only one game back, are destined to sit alone. Upon reflection, I wouldn't change that one bit. That's the American way.

Rewards are sweet and failure, well, John Fetzer has just died. This is his ghost speaking.

Oldtime Talk:

Charlie Gehringer: "Whenever I had a bad day, my mom would be sitting on the back porch when I got home from the ball park. She'd say to me: 'What's the matter? Aren't you trying anymore?'"

Hank Greenberg: "Charlie Gehringer never had a bad day."

Sonny Eliot, the Wondrous Weatherman, considered himself an outfielder and always wanted to work out with the Tigers, so he went to manager Jimmie Dykes and asked for a chance.

"OK," said Dykes, "but under one condition. Any time you touch a ball, it has to take one bounce on the ground. We don't need any dead weathermen around here."

President John McHale of the Tigers estimates it will cost $3,400 per seat in Comerica Park. Spaces in the parking structure next to the stadium will be between $7,000 and $8,000.

Bill Rabe, longtime Tiger fan, was asked to name his favorite player.

He said: "I have no favorite because when I went to Tiger Stadium to see Babe Ruth hit a home run when I was a boy, and he didn't hit one and I've spent half my time since then playing potsy in the grass."

Sparky Anderson was checking into a hotel. He wasn't paying for it but asked the desk clerk how much his room would cost.

She said: "It's $129 a night but it will be $159 tomorrow night."

"What's going to happen?" said Sparky. "Is the bathtub going to get bigger? Will the soap smell sweeter? Will I get an extra pillow?"

"No," said the woman. "But it will be April Fool's Day."

It was a quiet day in Tiger Stadium, so it seemed like a good time to interview outfielder Dick Sharon.

Question: How come you're wearing No. 27?"

Answer: "That's the one they gave me."

Q: What number did you want?

A: "I wanted No. 13 but I have this terrible affliction. I suffer from Tristie die ta phobia."

Q: What's that?

A: "It's the fear of No. 13. It's also the fear of backing into doorknobs."

Q: What's the most doorknobs you backed into in one season?

A: "Sixty-six . . . in the Texas League."

Q: What's your favorite food?

A: "Lutefisk."

Q: Lutefisk?

A: "It's a Norwegian codfish. You eat it with Lefsa."

Q: Who's your favorite musician?

A: "Beethoven."

Q: You're kidding?

A: "No, he wrote his last four whatever you call them while he was deaf. George Washington also had wooden teeth."

I'm leaving early. Can you get me out?

What goes on in the dressing room on a rainy night at Tiger Stadium:

Tom Brookens: "What two countries are connected by the Ambassador Bridge?"

Dave LaPoint: "I don't know."

Tom Gage: "One of them is Canada."

Dan Petry: "What's the other one?"

Coach Wally Moses came bouncing up the dugout steps and looked around at the new RFK Stadium in Washington.

"Sure doesn't remind me of old Griffith Stadium," he said.

"Whatever became of Griffith Stadium?" asked Hank Aguirre.

"They tore it down and built slums," said Jim Northrup.

Ernie Harwell likes to tell this story when he is giving a speech:

"One time the Brooklyn Dodgers were staying at a hotel in Cincinnati. They had a pitcher on the team named Elmer Sexhauer. One of the Cincinnati writers wanted to talk to him for a story and called him on the phone from his office.

"When the telephone operator answered the phone, the writer said: 'Do you have a Sexhauer at your hotel?' And she said: 'Hey, we don't even have enough time for a five-minute coffee break.'"

Bill Dewitt ran the Tigers for one year–1960. He liked to think of himself as an innovative operator. So, he had them shoot off fireworks after the Friday night games.

Good idea . . . until a runaway rocket set fire to a house in Corktown and the fireman had to put it out. End of the fireworks for Mr. D.

Jack Morris*: It was the late 1970s and I was pretty new with the team. I think the only reason they kept me was because manager Ralph Houk liked me. Mark Fidrych was supposed to pitch that night but 20 minutes before the game, one of the coaches came up to me and said: "Get your spikes on–you're going to start." I looked at him like he was crazy. "I'm not pitching, Bird is pitching." He said Fidrych was hurting and couldn't make it.*

So, I put my spikes on but how do you get ready in 20 minutes? They must have had 40,000 or 45,000 in the park to see Mark and when I started down to the bullpen, the public address announcer said: "Attention, please, Mark Fidrych is unable to pitch tonight. The pitcher will be Jack Morris."

You should have heard the booes. It was the first time I was booed in Tiger Stadium but not the last. I beat Texas that night but that didn't seem to matter.

The Longest Day

The game started at 1:30 p.m. It ended seven hours later. It was the longest game in the history of baseball.

By far.

The Tigers and Yankees went 22 innings on that memorable Sunday, June 24, 1962. The Yankees finally won 9-7. They played so long that the Michigan labor laws made them shut down the concession stands at 8:15 because women were not permitted to work more than 10 hours on a Sunday.

Matt Dennis, a sports writer for the Windsor Star, got up from his seat in the press box in the 18th inning and announced: "I've got to leave - my visa just expired."

The old record was nine hours and 19 minutes, so the Tigers and Yankees shattered the old record by one hour and 41 minutes.

The next day the Hall of Fame called Joe Falls, who was the official scorer of the game, and asked for a copy of the official box score, his story of the game, his picture and a tape of his voice recounting the unusual events of the day.

Hey, I figured my place was fixed forever in the lore and legend of baseball.

Until two years later - on May 31, 1964 - the New York Giants and San Francisco Giants played a 23-inning game that went seven hours and 43 minutes and the curators at Cooperstown took -
My box score . . .
My story . . .
My picture . . .
My voice . . .
And put them all into a small box and stored them in the basement of the Hall of Fame.

Nicknames of former Tigers:

"Hooks" Dauss

"Snooks" Dowd

"Piano Legs" Hickman

"Baby Doll" Jacobson

"Razor" Ledbetter

"Baldy" Louden

"Slim" Love

"Soldier Boy" Murphy

"Stubby" Overmire.

"Muddy" Ruel

"Hack" Simmons

"Phenomenal" Smith

"Tubby" Spener

"Sailor" Stroud

"Icehouse" Wilson

"Mutt" Wilson

"Squanto" Wilson

Quote-Unquote:

Richie Hebner, the grave digger: "I'm pretty good at digging graves. In 10 years, nobody has ever dug himself out of one yet."

The Penny Pincher

Hank Aguirre, the Merry Mexican, remembers standing in front of Jim Campbell's desk in Tiger Stadium pleading for a raise. Campbell, general manager of the Tigers, told him he was going to pay him the exact amount as the previous season.

Aguirre was mad. He gave Campbell a piece of his mind and started out of the office. He paused at the door.

"OK, I'll make you a deal," said Aguirre. "I'll sign the contract, but you've got to give me a raise. Make it a penny more than last year and I'm in.

Campbell called for his secretary. He told her: "Give Hank a new contract - for a penny raise."

Aguirre left and Campbell never saw the impish smile on his face.

Mick Kelleher, a utility infielder, who never hit a home run: "What's one home run? You hit one and they want you to hit two."

THEODORE SAMUEL WILLIAMS
"TED"
BOSTON RED SOX A.L. 1939-1960
BATTED .406 IN 1941. LED A.L. IN BATTING
6 TIMES; SLUGGING PERCENTAGE 9 TIMES;
TOTAL BASES 6 TIMES; RUNS SCORED 6 TIMES;
BASES ON BALLS 8 TIMES. TOTAL HITS 2654
INCLUDED 521 HOME RUNS. LIFETIME BATTING
AVERAGE .344; LIFETIME SLUGGING AVERAGE
.634 MOST VALUABLE A.L. PLAYER 1946 & 1949.
PLAYED IN 18 ALL STAR GAMES, NAMED PLAYER
OF THE DECADE 1951-1960.

Little Known Fact: The Tigers once mulled a trade of Al Kaline for Ted Williams. The Red Sox made the offer and Jim Campbell and Rick Ferrell thought it over, finally rejecting the deal because Williams was more than 10 years older than Kaline.

Ted Williams, *former Boston Red Sox outfielder: Tiger Stadium was a great place to hit and the best thing about it is that the Tigers had some great pitchers in those days. Hal Newhouser, Dizzy Trout, Virgil Trucks. They would come right at you and even though they had great stuff, they put the ball where you could get at it. There was none of this "dilly dallying" around. I only wish I could have faced Schoolboy Rowe. They say he was something else.*

The first time I saw the park I looked around at all the green seats and somebody pointed to the third deck in rightfield and said Jim Bottomley hit one up there. The first time up that day, I hit one up there, too, and the next day I hit one over the roof. They told me later I was the first one to do it. I guess the year was 1939.

Most people talk about the home run I hit in the 1941 All-Star Game. It came with two out in the ninth and won the game. But it was an embarrassing moment for me. As I went around the bases, I was jumping up and down and clapping my hands. I didn't realize it at the moment because I was so happy, but when I saw myself a few days later in the Movietone News in a theater, I was shocked. I said, "My God, I'll never do that again." Now they all do it, but times are different.

I've always loved Detroit, especially the sports writers.
(Really?)

LIGHTS On, EVERYBODY

Who said the Tigers were a conservative organization? They were the next-to-last team (Boston was last) in signing a black player, and the last team in the American League to install lights.

The first night game in Tiger Stadium took place on June 15, 1948. This was 13 years after the lights first went up in Cincinnati. And they had no idea how to go about it.

They knew so little about lights they did not start the game until 9:30. They didn't think they'd take effect until it was almost completely dark.

They opened the gates at 6 p.m. and people started pouring through the gates. The Tigers staged several contests on the field to pass the time.

Finally, at 9:28, the lights were turned on and the crowd let out a spontaneous "Oooooooooh!"

Hal Newhouser beat the Philadel-

phia A's 4-1 and the next day columnist Lyall Smith wrote in *The Detroit Free Press*: "For some reason I can't explain, all the action looks faster under the lights. Runners appear to rip down the base lines faster than in the afternoon. Every ball that starts out seems headed for the seats.

"Maybe an ocultist or psychiatrist can explain this optical illusion."

This is not the Rockettes chorus line. not even close.

Cobbisms:

"A bat is a wondrous weapon."

••••

"The baseline belongs to me."

••••

Cobb pitched three times for the Tigers - twice in 1918 and once in 1925. He worked a total of five innings, allowing six hits, and was credited with saving one game.

••••

Cobb was paid $1,500 in his first year with the Tigers.

The immortal Tito Fuentes: "The pitchers shouldn't throw at me. I'm the father of five or six children."

Rocky Bridges, former shortstop of the Tigers, was once asked to enter a cow milking contest in his home town of Refugio, Tex.

He said: "I didn't try too hard. I finished second. I was afraid I'd get emotionally involved with the cow."

Let's have a moment of silence for Francis Sigafoos, who played 14 games for the Tigers in 1929.

He smacked a home run into the leftfield seats but the umpires made him come back and do it again. They ruled the pitcher had committed a balk before throwing the ball.

The home run was wiped out and poor Siggy never hit another one.

Hank Aguirre speaking:

"Did you hear the one about the guy who went to see his doctor and the doctor examined him and told him: 'I've got good news and bad news for you.'

"The guy said: 'Give me the bad news first.'

"The doctor said: 'I have to amputate your right leg.'

"'What's the good news?'

"'I shot a hole in one last week,'" said the doctor."

a time when Joe Falls was a star of stage, screen and radio. Well, radio, anyway.

How's this for a triple play?

Lou Berberet was not a pretty player. The former catcher, in fact, looked a little ragged in and out of uniform. Nobody ever paid him any compliments.

One day a young boy spoke to him in spring training and said: "Mr. Berberet, my sister thinks you are one of the best catchers in baseball. She just loves watching you play."

Berberet smiled. "Isn't that nice," he said. "How old is she?"

The boy said: "Three."

Rocky Bridges loved to go to Windsor and visit the bars.

"Neat place," he would say. "You can get some great imported beer over there, like Budweiser."

Wally Moses, a former coach of the Tigers, was talking about the greatest ovation he ever heard in his life.

It happened near the end of his career as a player. As he was stepping to the plate in Yankee Stadium, the fans gave out with a rousing cheer.

But, lo, it wasn't for old Wally.

The guy on the public address microphone had just said: "Ladies and gentlemen, your attention, please. Benito Mussolini, the Italian dictator, has just been put to death in Italy by execution."

Enos Cabell was considered the spiritual leader of the Tigers, so he decided to throw a party for his teammates in their hotel in Minneapolis. He rented three rooms.

The guys came in and ate up $1,600 in eats and drinks.

"My last party," said Cabell.

Former shortstop Rocky Bridges, ever the imp, wondered: "If we go to the metric system, what will they call dog pounds?"

Walt Terrell was an honest guy when he pitched for the Tigers.

He was asked how tough it was keeping the ball in Tiger Stadium when he was on the mound.

"Hey, I have trouble keeping the ball in the city."

Hey, put the umbrella away. It's not raining.

Two more classics from Sparky Anderson:

1. "If you lose, you don't win."

2. "Pain doesn't hurt."

The Tigers used to hold a Kangaroo Court and fine each other for mistakes on and off the field. Sparky Anderson was fined $10 for wearing a tie on the team bus.

He asked: "Do Kangaroos ever hold People Court?"

Mickey Tettleton, the ex-catcher, was asked the name of his first girlfriend.

He replied: "I never had a first girlfriend."

One minute with Skeeter Barnes, one of our all-time favorite players on the Tigers:

Q: What was your first job?

A: "You mean other than raking leaves or shoveling snow? I worked in a barber shop as a shoeshine boy. I was 12 years old and they thought I was old enough to sweep up the hair off the floor."

Q: First girlfriend?

A. "Her name was Lenny. I liked her for two reasons. She was so good looking and she kept my statistics during the baseball season."

Q: A special treat?

A: "Grapes. I love grapes. Green grapes. Seedless. I can never get burned out on grapes. I can sit down and eat them until there are none left."

Q: Best vacation?

A: "I never had a vacation."

Q: Rain?

A: "I don't like it because when it rains, all I can do is watch it."

Can you squeeze some popcorn through the fence?

Alex Grammas, former third base coach under Sparky Anderson, was asked for his strongest memory of spring training.

"It was the day I picked up the paper and it was April 4th," said Grammas. "I said to myself, 'Well, I'll be . . . yesterday was my birthday.'"

Paul Gibson, a lefthanded reliever for the Tigers, was asked if he was a good cook.

He said: "I am a sensational cook. Hamburgers are my specialty. I put them on the grill and I take them off the grill."

Ty Cobb played his last game in an Oldtimer's Game in Yankee Stadium. He was 61 years old and they had him batting lead-off.

He took his place in the batter's box and as he was getting settled in, he turned to the catcher and said: "Would you mind moving back a bit. I haven't done this for a long time and I don't want to lose control of the bat and hit you with it."

The catcher moved back a few feet.

Cobb got set again.

"You know, I'm pretty nervous about this whole thing. Could you move back just a little more."

The catcher moved back a little more.

Cobb bunted the first pitch and beat it out for a hit.

Cecil Fielder on autographs: "I never got them, but I give them."

***Kirk Gibson**, former outfielder: You can look at this stadium and it says "Detroit." It has a ton of character. It's rough looking, it's tough looking. It's blue collar.*

The greatest fan I ever knew was a man who sat in the right centerfield bleachers when I came up as a rookie in 1979, He was at every game and he used to call me "SLUGGER!" He'd yell at Sparky, "HEY, SPARK!" He'd call Lou Whitaker out there and yell, "HEY, SWEETNESS!" We all went out there, and here was a guy who paid the usher to get in there every day. He never bought a ticket. That's how it used to be in the old ball park. He didn't want to sit in the Tiger Den seats. He wanted to be in the lower right-centerfield bleachers and he'd let us know he was there, He'd be there for BP and he was just an ordinary guy.

That's the beauty of Tiger Stadium, that so many different kinds of people can get together and enjoy themselves. I think Detroit has a personality of its own. If you go around and ask people if they would like to live here, they would say "no." But we all choose to live here and there is a reason for it. We see what Detroit has to offer. We have a lot of personality, a lot of character. We have the ability to see the beauty around us. We've worked together. We're hard-working people.

Detroit's gotten a bad rap, but we're all working together to prove to everyone in the country that not only is it not a bad place to live, but pay attention and maybe you'll learn something.

COHEN'S CORNER

The Reggie Tower. The light tower Reggie Jackson hit in the 1971 All-Star Game. You cannot see the dent in the transformer.

right-hander and sent the tennis ball screaming off the transformer - a blast estimated at 212 feet. He did not renegotiate his contract.

Only one man in history ever counted every seat in Tiger Stadium - our man, Irwin. This was when he was the director of group ticket sales and, lo and behold, he found seven seats the ticket office never knew about.

One was a lower box seat near the visitor's bullpen. The other six were upper reserve seats along the first base line. Irwin would be a good man at finding the loopholes in your income tax.

Only two men have ever hit the transformer on the light tower in rightcenter field in Tiger Stadium - Reggie Jackson and Irwin Cohen.

Reggie did it in the 1971 All-Star Game and Irwin during a family picnic on the grass in rightfield. In those days, employees of the Tigers and their families were allowed to use the field when the Tigers were out of town.

Irwin stood in rightfield and connected off a nine-year-old

TWO ROOFTOP STADIUM SLUGGERS
- *Reggie Jackson and Irwin Cohen*

On a late mid-week afternoon, Irwin walked past the second floor employee dining room and spotted a body on the floor.

He went for a phone and called 911 as he walked toward the motionless body.

"Call 'em back and tell them not to come," said the familiar voice on the floor of the darkened room.

Woman at work. It is Heather Nabozny, the new head grounds-keeper. She must do a great job of vacuuming at home.

"I always try to take a nap on the floor before a night game because of my back," explained Ernie Harwell.

Frank Fenick, *former grounds-keeper: When Kirk Gibson first came up, they put him in rightfield and he wasn't too good with the glove, and he didn't have much of an arm. One day he asked me if I could let the grass grow a little longer out there so when the ball came to him, it would slow down and come to a stop and all he had to do was pick it up and throw it back to the infield.*

But Charlie Silvera's teeth really got to me. Charlie was a coach and he was having trouble with his uppers. He put them into his pocket one day when he was running around shagging balls and they fell out. I guess he didn't miss them until he woke up the next morning. And now here he is running across the outfield grass at about 6 a.m. and he is screaming: "DON'T CUT THE GRASS! DON'T CUT THE GRASS!"

We were playing a day game and he knew we'd be out there early with our mowers.

He told me how much the teeth cost him, so now we had all the boys on their hands and knees looking for them. We found them and I thought Charlie was going to give me a hug.

Look at the guy in the 22nd row. He's got his hand on her knee.

Ty Cobb once went 0-for-32 but didn't talk about it. Nobody asked him about it, either.

Richie Hebner, the celebrated grave digger: "The absolute worst grave diggers in the world are at Forest Lawn. Those guys wear tuxedos."

Don't leave. Easley, Higgy and Clark are coming up in the bottom of the ninth.

Milt Wilcox's favorite ball park was Memorial Stadium in Baltimore: "Great pinball machine in the clubhouse."

Sonny Eliot notes that on July 3, 1906, Germany Schaefer of the Tigers played one inning in a raincoat against the Cleveland Indians. Why not? It was raining.

Sparky Speaks:

"I like the trading cards better since they took my playing record off the back and put on my managerial record."

The night the Yankees won the 1928 pennant in Detroit, Babe Ruth wanted to throw a party and asked the hotel if it could get him a piano. The hotel said no, so The Babe went out and bought one.

After Alan Trammell hit a grand slam off Dan Quizenberry of the Kansas city Royals, Quizenberry said: "That's a longer ground ball than I usually give up."

Coach Dick Tracewski's favorite shopping city was New York.

"I loved it along Delancy Street in lower Manhattan," he said. "You can buy anything there, from grapefruits to sneakers. There's nothing like eating grapefruits in your sneakers."

Hank Aguirre: "If lefthanded pitchers are called "Southpaws," why aren't right-handed pitchers called "Northpaws?""

Tom Brookens, the quiet third baseman, said: "The toughest job I ever had was looking for a job."

Stat: Darrell Evans hit his 300th home run at 3 p.m. on a 3-0 count.

Did you know Frank Howard's over-the-roof shot hit the leftfield roof in Tiger Stadium and bounced on the field?

Tom Gage, *Detroit News baseball writer: The time I love Tiger Stadium the most is when I'm done working and I don't take the elevator down. I take the steps instead. The place is empty and it's absolutely beautiful. But it's time. It has had a good run but it's a little rickety now.*

When I was a kid, I used to play baseball board games with spinners and then write little stories about what happened. I'm probably doing the job I always wanted to do.

Tom Gage, Detroit's senior baseball writer: He is trying to out-write Joe Falls, which isn't hard to do.

My favorite place to sit as a kid was in the overhang in rightfield. That's where a lot of the home runs go. The only ball I ever got was when Gates Brown hit one through the exit and I was standing in line to get a hot dog and the ball rolled right to me.

Joe Meets Hank

I

The first time I met Hank Greenberg was in my rookie year as a baseball writer in 1956. I wasn't quite sure how to go about my job. It probably sounds silly, but there can be a lot to learn on the daily baseball beat besides writing and reporting. When to send out your laundry. When does the bus leave, and from where? How much do you tip? In fact, where do you eat? Where do you sit on the plane?

The Tigers were playing the White Sox in Chicago and after making the usual trip to both dressing rooms and dugouts, the guys started going upstairs to the Bard's Room for lunch.

What was the Bard's room? I didn't want to ask because I was trying hard not to be a rookie. After they left, I asked a couple of ushers and they told me how to get to the press room.

I walked in and the place was jammed. It looked like a big saloon. Guys were standing at the bar. Others were sitting at tables, eating. Everyone was talking and the noise was, well, like it gets in saloons.

I saw an empty table in a corner and sat down. I didn't drink, so I wasn't going to the bar, and I didn't know how to get any food. Do they take your order? Or do they have it laid out on a table? I didn't know, so I took out my scorebook and pretended to read it.

"Hi!"

I looked up.

Hank Greenberg was hovering over my table. I knew him from all the pictures and films and knew he was involved with Bill Veeck in running the White Sox.

"I'm Hank Greenberg. You're Joe Falls, the new writer on the Detroit Times. Welcome to

Our beloved Sarah, the press box elevator lady. The writers say if the Tigers don't take her to Comerica Park, they're not going.

Chicago. Would you like to join me for lunch?"

I extended my hand and said, "Thank you. It's nice of you to invite me."

He took me across the room, but not before introducing me to everyone along the way. I could not hope to know who they all were, or even what they did, but I could see the smile on Greenberg's face as he made each introduction.

II

The last time I met Hank, he was into his 70s. The Tigers were going to have a day for him and Charlie Gehringer - the G-Men from the 1930s. So I went to Los Angeles, where Greenberg lived, and took photographer Doc Holcomb with me so we could do a Sunday layout.

He told us to meet him at his tennis club. I believe it was in Beverly Hills.

It was the middle of the afternoon when we got there and the match was going hot and heavy. The club was in a tree-lined neighborhood and almost everything was covered with shade.

The G-Men say goodbye: The day they retired the numbers of Charlie Gehringer (2) and High Henry Greenberg (5) in 1983.

Hank was wearing white shorts and a white shirt and a blue Los Angeles Dodgers cap, pulled down tightly over his head. They were playing doubles.

We sat down quietly. He didn't see us.

The look on his face as he played - how can I describe it? One of intensity? Yes. Determination? Yes. Concentration? Yes. Being a poor poet, I thought, "Geez, this is how he must have been when he played for the Tigers." I thought of all those days - those mornings - when he would go out to the ball park by himself, round up some neighborhood kids, and take batting practice until the callouses on his hands would bleed.

He played each point as if it were the most important point of his life. And, each time, he would lose a point - through a mistake or otherwise - he would let out a loud expletive.

He was cussing himself out.

I guess I was smiling.

What got me were his legs. They were old and wrinkled, as legs are supposed to do. But the skin above his knees was loose and flabby, and hung down over his knees.

What? No pickle relish?

Then he saw us, Doc and I sitting on a bench against a vine-covered wall.

"TIME!" he called out, and walked over to us. He shook our hands and smiled brightly and said it was good to see us. (What happened to that demon on the court?)

He called out a name, and a man - a waiter - appeared from behind some bushes.

"Yes, sir?"

"These are my friends, my friends from Detroit," Greenberg said. "Please put them at the umbrella table and take their order. Drinks, lunch, whatever they want."

Greenberg looked at us.

"Please enjoy yourself. I won't be much longer. Please have what you want and I'll join you after we polish off these guys."

He went back to the court.

"OK, you guys ... let's see your best game. I haven't seen it yet."

The other three men laughed. One said, "Your serve, Henry."

Frank Beckmann, *WJR broadcaster: It didn't hit me until opening day this year how much of my life had revolved aound Tiger Stadium – almost like bookmarks in my career. I went there with my mother and father and learned to love baseball . . . Sunday doubleheaders . . .Charlie Maxwell, old Paw Paw . . .green seats, sunny days and blue skies.*

I used to go there on Lutheran Night and be out on the field with the other kids from the Mel Ott League. We were allowed to run out to the flagpole and stand on the field for the national anthem.

It was at Tiger Stadium where I found out I needed glasses. My mother saw me squinting at the scoreboard. One of my first jobs as a kid was dusting off the seats. They were all great days.

This has nothing to do with Tiger Stadium but it is too good to pass up. The greatest 1-2-3 finish in the history of horse racing took place at the Detroit Race Course in 1953:

1. Fun for Two

2. I'm Expecting

3. Sandra's Baby

What the execs eat. Where are the hot dogs?

What did Tiger Stadium mean to Champ Summers?

"It's like going out for a steak," he said. "If there is no atmosphere in the place, I don't enjoy my steak. I always enjoyed Tiger Stadium. Tiger Stadium is a steak."

Time for lunch, anyone not eating pizza can leave.

Mickey Lolich won a ball game and bought nine pizzas for his teammates to eat in the clubouse.

"Not too smart," said one of the writers. "You saved nothing for the press."

"Very smart," said Lolich. "I sent a pizza in to the umpires."

April 8, 1979 was a significant date in the history of Tiger Stadium. That was the day the first woman reporter went into the Tigers' dressing room. It was Gail Granik, a sportscaster from Ch. 4 in Detroit.

She moved deliberately around the dressing room with her camera crew and interviewed Dave Rozema (fully clothed), Steve Kemp (swimming shorts) and Ron LeFlore (undershirt, undershorts and and baseball cap.)

When Norm Cash and Hank Aguirre broke in as color commentators on the Tiger telecasts, they wondered what would happen to the ratings.

"They'll go up," said Aguirre. "I've got a female cat, a female dog, a wife and three daughters."

Could you pass the screen test from the upper deck in right?

Alan Trammell was talking about life on the road with the Tigers.

"All those years, I brought my dominoes with me on the planes," he said. "I don't know why I did it. Nobody ever played with me."

When Leon Wagner - old "Daddy Wags" - came into Tiger Stadium with the Los Angeles Angels for a weekend series against the Tigers, he was grumbling about sharing his outfield job with another player.

He said: "I don't care for this pontoon system."

No, Godzilla didn't come to today's game.

Rusty Staub was holding out one season and told general manager Jim Campbell he would sign under three conditions:

1. The Tigers retire the rest of a personal loan - estimated at $36,000.

2. They pay off the mortgage on his house in Houston - a figure of around $55,000.

3. They pay his mother $500 a month for the next five years - a package of 30,000.

Campbell was unavailable for comment.

When outfielder Don Demeter was asked for his autograph, he would sign: "Wm. Cody."

He said: "I figured Buffalo Bill never got enough credit for what he did."

Ernie Harwell has been broadcasting baseball for 123 years - or something like it. He was asked to pick his all-time team from the hometown players he saw while working in the broadcast booth:

1B - Norm Cash, Tigers

2B - Jackie Robinson,
Brooklyn Dodgers

SS - Pee Wee Reese, Dodgers, and
Alan Trammell, Tigers

3B - Brooks Robinson, Orioles

RF - Al Kaline, Tigers

CF - Willie Mays,
New York Giants

LF - Willie Horton, Tigers

C - Roy Campanella,
Brooklyn Dodgers

RHP - Denny McLain, Tigers

LHP - Mickey Lolich, Tigers

Manager - Sparky Anderson,
Tigers, and Leo Durocher, Giants

Donald Davidson, the diminutive traveling secretary of the Atlanta Braves, stopped off at Tiger Stadium to check on the hotels and press facilities.

He stood 48 inches high.

When asked about his height, he said: "I can do anything any normal-sized person can do. I can drive a car and sit on a bar stool. I just can't reach the elevator button if I'm higher than the 10th floor."

***Tony Clark**, first baseman: The most exciting time for me was the first night I came up. I had an opportunity to look around the park and could see all the dents in the wall and the scrapes in the paint. I wondered who did all that, and then I thought of all the great players who hit home runs in Tiger Stadium, Babe Ruth, Reggie Jackson, all of them.*

We were playing the Cleveland Indians one night and Eddie Murray drew a walk and now here he comes down to first base. I'm a switch hitter and now here is one of the greatest switch hitters of all time trotting right toward me. I didn't know what to do or what to say. So, when he got there, all I said was: "Hello, Mr. Murray."

Quote-Unquote:

GEORGE CLYDE KELL
PHILADELPHIA A. L. 1943 - 1946
DETROIT A. L. 1946 - 1952
BOSTON A. L. 1952 - 1954
CHICAGO A. L. 1954 - 1956
BALTIMORE A. L. 1956 - 1957
PREMIER A. L. THIRD BASEMAN OF 1940'S AND
1950'S. SOLID HITTER AND SURE-HANDED FIELDER
WITH STRONG, ACCURATE ARM. BATTED OVER
.300 9 TIMES, LEADING LEAGUE WITH .343 IN
1949. LED A. L. THIRD BASEMEN IN FIELDING
PCT. 7 TIMES, ASSISTS 4 TIMES AND PUTOUTS
AND DOUBLE PLAYS TWICE.

A tornado was ripping through the suburbs of Kansas City. Everything was blowing around in the ball park - including the tar paper off the roof of the stadium - and the Tigers-A's game was halted as the skies darkened, the rains fell and the winds picked up.

Baseball writer George Cantor got up from his seat in the press box and went down to the broadcast booth and asked George Kell if he could sit next to him.

"Sure," said Kell. "But why?"

Cantor said: "As far as I know, nobody has ever been killed by a tornado while broadcasting a major league baseball game."

Rocky Bridges - "The manager of the Walla Walla team is Steve Ditto."

Enos Cabell said it: "We don't have any hitters, so how can we have a designated hitter?"

Norm Cash knocked the ball over the rightfield roof and an unnamed sports writer wrote: "The ball hit a police toe truck on Trumbull Ave."

Worse yet, his paper printed it that way.

Babe Ruth hit the longest home run in Tiger Stadium history. He connected off Lil Stoner of the Tigers in 1926.

The ball traveled 620 feet. It cleared the rightfield fence and rolled to a halt at the intersection of Cherry Street. Believe it. H.G. Salsinger, longtime sports editor of The Detroit News, went out into the street to measure it.

Catcher John Sullivan had a rather inauspicious debut in the major leagues. He broke in with the Tigers when they opened the season in Kansas City in 1963.

As he went to the plate to take the warmup throws from the pitcher in the bottom of the first inning, a pigeon flew overhead and - splaaaat! - left Sullivan a message on his cap, his shoulders and his glove.

It was a big series in Toronto and when Jack Morris came bouncing up the dugout steps before the first game, there were five TV men asking him for an interview.

Before they could ask a question, Morris said: "Hi, everybody! This is the biggest series in the history of baseball. If we lose, we are finished for all time. If he win, we're the World Champions again. Thank you and goodbye."

Speaking of pigeons, Willie Horton was at the plate in Fenway Park in Boston when he fouled one up into the air at home plate.

The ball hit a pigeon and the bird fell smack on the plate, sending Willie backing away in terror.

Hey Kid. It costs more to park than to get into the park.

John McHale, Jr., president of the Tigers: My father became general manager in 1957 and served until 1959. He and my mother treated a trip to Tiger Stadium as a special occasion. They would take us kids four or five times a year and it was a great experience.

We would come up the back elevator and try to behave as well as we could. We'd move with my father through the front offices and down into the stands. The overwhelming impression was the great, expansive green grass surrounded by this courtyard of green seats, topped off by the Delco sign on the scoreboard in centerfield which lit up when home runs were hit.

Losing this ball park is like the passing of a relative.

Please take off your hats if you don't like the manager.

The Babe's 700th

The big moment took place in Tiger Stadium on July 13, 1934. It was Babe Ruth's last year in baseball.

He hit more homers in the Detroit ball park than any other visiting player - 60 of them - and this one was special.

With Tommy Bridges on the mound for the Tigers, Ruth sent the ball over the rightfield wall and it rolled two blocks away to Plum Street.

He knew what the home run meant and as he rounded first base, he called out: "That's No. 700 for me! Get me that ball! I'll pay 50 smackers for it."

A young man of 17 retrieved the ball and Ruth rewarded him with a new $20 bill, which he borrowed from manager Joe McCarthy.

no. 1

The first home run hit in Tiger Stadium - then Navin Field - came off the bat of rookie second baseman Del Pratt of the St. Louis Browns on May 5, 1912. It came in the 11th game played at Navin Field.

He connected off pitcher Ed Willert and the ball took a freak bounce off the left-centerfield wall and fell behind the scoreboard, where it could not be retrieved.

On June 10, shortstop Donie Bush became the first Tiger to homer in Navin Field when he cracked an inside-the-park home run. Frank (Home Run) Baker of the Philadelphia A's became the first player to clear the fences five days later.

Gates Brown*, former out-fielder: When I was incarcerated in Ohio as a young man, I read a lot of books about Tiger Stadium. Ty Cobb, Heinie Manush, Hank Greenberg, all of them.*

God, how I loved that rightfield overhang. I just wish I could have played a little more. It was a good place to hit, and I'm proud to say I was one of the first black players to play for the Tigers.

I also take pride in the fact that I was on the 1968 and 1984 champions - first, as a player, then as a coach. Dick Tracewski did the same thing and we were friends for years.

The most memorable day was the day we beat the Red Sox in a doubleheader in Tiger Stadium and I got the winning hits in both games. I can still hear that sellout crowd going crazy.

Before he left us, Hank Aguirre, the Merry Mexican, left us with some smiles:

• "You know you're getting old when you feel your corns more than your oats."

• "Marriage is the most expensive way to discover your faults."

• "If radio is the mother of television, who is the father?"

• "Why do so many baseball teams become 'The Boys of Slumber.'

• "Beware of women with wash-and-wear wedding dresses."

• "Paying alimony is like pumping gas into another man's tank."

(Miss you, big guy)

This is where Al Benton used to warm up in the old days. No, that's not Al Benton leaning on the batting cage.

Mark Fidrych, *former pitcher: I'd love to step out on the field one more time. Actually, what I'd like to do is slip into the stadium around midnight when nobody is around. I'd like to get past security and steal the pitcher's mound. They'd wake up in the morning and wonder what happened.*

I can't help myself . . . I still think of all those wonderful days I was out there. I'd like to be like Mickey Stanley that year they tore up the whole field to put in a new one. He hired a truck and took all the grass to a new house he was building.

I'd love to have the pitcher's mound in my back yard.

Please get off the field. We have a game to play.

Quotable:

Gates Brown, the premier pinch hitter, when asked what his buddy, Willie Horton, took in school: "Willie took algebra, English, history and overcoats."

Ike Brown, the happy-go lucky bench warmer: "I am our Designated Sitter."

Manager Jimmy Dykes, on pitcher Pete Burnside running for an hour after practice: "If you do it with your legs instead of your arm, this guy would be a 30-game winner."

Max Lapides, fan: My father was old enough to remember the start of the American League in 1900. I probably spent more time in the ballpark with my father than most kids spend with their father in a lifetime. We went to weekend games and then, when they put in lights, we used to go in the middle of the week–60 times a year. The ballpark really means my father.

I go back to Navin Field. I remember the Sunday doubleheaders with the overflow crowds, standing, roped off in the outfield. The gentlemen stood out there in the hot sun with their shirts, ties and straw hats on.

Growing up as a jewish kid in Detroit, Hank Greenberg was so important to us. World War II was raging and anti-semitism was rampant in Germany, and Hank gave us a real reason to be proud of our religion.

Dave Bergman, *former first baseman: Everybody talks about the night in 1987 when I hit a game-winning homer off Toronto in the 10th inning after fouling off 13 pitches - the last seven in a row on a 3-2 count. As time goes on, that story gets better and better, as if I caught a fish and it got larger and larger.*

Because of my talent level, I was never going to be a superstar. I was just someone who plugged in the little cracks here and there. Leroy Jackson was pitching and we went back a long way together, teammates in winter ball.

He kept challenging me and neither was going to give in. I knew it wasn't going to end up as a walk. I kept swinging and closing my eyes. That's what I always did. I'd swing and close my eyes.

He finally threw me a slider, down and in. It was a nasty pitch. I closed my eyes and the ball landed in the seats. To this day, my mom is disappointed because I didn't do cartwheels around the bases. I was just a boring player.

What's the matter? Don't these guys talk to each other?

Quotable:

Sparky Anderson's five rules for handling the pressure of publicity:

1. Order room service whenever possible.

2. Don't answer your phone. Live by the red message light.

3. Stay out of lobbies and dining rooms.

4. Don't be rude to people but keep walking if they besiege you for autographs.

5. Don't miss the team bus.

Inside
Tiger Stadium

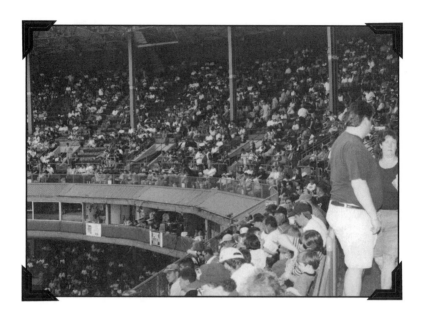

Outside

Tiger Stadium

WELCOME

A FEW DAYS IN THE LIFE OF
SPARKY ANDERSON

(Sunday Afternoon)

The game is over and he hears the fans in Tiger Stadium clamoring, calling out his name as he starts up the tunnel to the clubhouse.

"Sparky! Sparky! Sparky!"

It is near the end of the 1987 season. The Tigers have won an important game and the fans are asking him to come back out on the field. He feels a rush of embarrassment but stops in his tracks.

"Sparky! Sparky! Sparky!"

He turns around and bounds up the dugout steps. He faces the stands and doffs his cap. The roars get louder. Then he goes down the steps and is gone from sight. Nobody notices but there is no smile on his face.

(Sunday Night)

It is two hours later and Sparky is sitting in a Mexican restaurant near the ball park. He is with his wife, Carol, his son, Al, and his coach, Billy Consolo. Consolo is Sparky's best friend and is living with him in Sparky's

house in Bloomfield Hills.

Sparky says to his son, "Hey, Al, were you cheering for me like everyone else?"

The young man stirs in his chair.

His mother says, "Yes, he was cheering like everyone else. He was applauding like everyone else. When he realized they were calling out your name, he stopped applauding and sat down."

These prices are sky high.

"That's my son," said Sparky. "A man of taste."

Sparky orders a chicken taco and a cheese enchilada. They are his favorites. He also orders a steak, cooked in lemon and garlic and covered with onions. "This is heaven," he says.

The owner comes to the table. "This one is on the players," he says. "They just called and want to pick up the check."

Sparky wipes his mouth and looks over from the top of his napkin.

"Thank you, my man," he says. "I thank you for your thought, but I have been around the block a few times. You put that check right down here and I will take care of it."

The owner looks at him and smiles.

(Monday Morning)

Sparky knows the phone will ring about 7:40. That's when J.P. McCarthy of radio station WJR will be calling. He calls almost every morning to chat with the Detroit manager.

Sparky pulls his thoughts together and is ready when the phone rings.

They talk for five minutes. He hangs up and lights his pipe. He lies back on the pillow and looks up at the ceiling. Nice ceiling, he thinks. Good paint job.

He drives to the ball park with Consolo. He goes up to Jim Campbell's office. Campbell is sitting behind his desk. Sparky walks in and says, "How'd you like what those fans did yesterday, giving me that big ovation?"

"Not bad," says Campbell.

Here's a lady with a real change up.

"What I should have done," said Sparky, "is gone out to the middle of the mound and raised my hands like Julius Caesar and let them get a really good look at me. I mean, that was a great body they were seeing out there yesterday."

This young man is hanging on, just like his favorite team.

Campbell tells Sparky he'd better not miss the bus to the airport.

(Monday Afternoon)

Sparky is first off the team bus when it arrives at the hotel in Milwaukee. He walks into the lobby, where they have coffee, milk, soda pop and cookies set out for the team's arrival.

He picks up a couple of cans of Coke and two cookies and heads for his room. He figures they will make a nice snack for after the game. One hour later the cookies are gone.

(Tuesday Morning)

It is nine o'clock and Sparky is sitting in the corner booth of the coffee shop. He is wearing his jogging suit. It is raining.

Don Sutton, a Milwaukee pitcher, sits down at the next table.

"You ever see lightning like that last night?" Sutton asks.

"I think one bolt hit the loudspeakers," says Anderson. "It was the second loudest noise I ever heard in a ball park."

Sutton stares at him.

"You're not going to believe the first," says Sparky. "It happened in Dodger Stadium in 1970. "I'm with the Reds and Woody Woodward is our shortstop. He's standing out there and - BAM! - this puff of smoke goes right up into the air, right behind him. Do you know what it was?"

Sutton is still staring.

"It was a bag of flour," says Sparky. "A BAG OF FLOUR. Somebody drops the thing from an airplane and if it lands on Woodward, I mean he's gone. It kills him."

(Tuesday Afternoon)

Back in his room, Sparky turns on his TV set. He watches a replay of the Boston College-North Carolina football game. He doesn't like what he sees. Doug Flutie has four touchdown passes for Boston College. His coach keeps him on the field and pretty soon he has six touchdown passes.

Sparky turns off the TV set. He thinks to himself, "The Heisman Trophy, eh? Is that how they do it - they rub it in."

Sparky picks up the phone. He is checking in with "The King." That's what he calls Jim Campbell.

He says, "Hey, King. This is The Slob calling."

Campbell laughs. They talk about the team for 15 minutes,

Where the brass sit. That's John McHale at the right on the phone, asking how Comerica park is coming along.

then Sparky heads out to the ball park.

Marty Castillo, a utility infielder, asks if Sparky and his coaches will leave the clubhouse for a while. They want to talk over how to cut up the World Series shares.

"May I say a few words to the boys before I leave?" Sparky asks.

Castillo nods.

"Thank you," says Sparky.

The Detroit manager makes sure the dressing room door is closed. He gets the attention of the players. "You guys do what you want but I just want you to know how Johnny Bench handled things in Cincinnati," Sparky says. "He'd tell all the guys, 'Hey, men, this is free money. Let's make sure we share it with everybody.'"

Sparky walks out of the room. It is silent as he leaves.

(Wednesday Morning)

It is 11:45 and The AP photographer raps on the door of Sparky's hotel room in midtown Manhattan. He is there to do a picture story on the Detroit manager.

Sparky opens the door. "Come in, come in," he says to the photographer.

The room is small, just a bed and a dresser, and a few chairs. It was not what the photographer wanted to see. He needs a little room to do his work.

A phone rings somewhere in the distance.

"Man, there it goes again," says Sparky. "The guy next door sure has been getting a lot of calls. The phone is ringing and ringing."

The photographer tries the door between the rooms. It opens. He pokes his head in and sees a luxurious layout - sofas, easy chairs, drapes, two TV sets, a small dining room. A tray of sandwiches and a bowl of fruit are set out on a table. A magnum of champagne is sitting in a silver bucket.

"I think this is for you," says the photographer.

Sparky peeks in. "I'll be dammed," he says. "I didn't know I had two rooms."

(Wednesday Night)

It is almost midnight when the bus gets back to the hotel. Everyone gets off except one man. When they're all gone, Sparky says to the driver, "Okay, Josh, you know where to go."

The driver nods and pulls away into the night. Ten minutes later he pulls up in front of the Stage Deli. Sparky bows to him before he gets out. "Thank you, my man. I will see you tomorrow night."

The driver salutes him.

Sparky goes inside where two of his coaches - Consolo and Dick Tracewski - are waiting for him.

He orders a liverwurst sandwich on rye. He always orders a liverwurst sandwich on rye at the Stage Deli. They sit there until two o'clock in the morning talking baseball.

Sonny Eliot, weatherman: *Baseball is a great game. It's chess, it's checkers. It is a mind game for all involved. I went to Navin field when they had a green wall out in right field, plus a scoreboard. We'd hang around the Cherry Street entrance because a guy would come out and pick some of the kids to be ushers for the day. But you had to bring your own rag.*

My mother loved baseball but she didn't know anything about the game except Hank Greenberg played for the Tigers. She'd always ask me if he hit a home run.

One day she was listening to the radio and the announcer said the pitcher picked up the resin bag. My mother exclaimed: "Rosinbag? Is there another Jewish player on the team?"

SPARKYISMS

* "I don't know why the players make such a big deal out of sitting in first class on a plane. Does that mean they'll get there quicker?"

* "If I wasn't a manager, I'd be a house painter. I like to paint. I'm a good painter. You can't get into trouble when you paint. If you see something wrong, you can just paint over it."

* "The only thing a manager can do once the game starts is to make moves with his pitchers, and you are going to be good at that only if you have good pitchers."

* "I understand people who boo us. It's like going to a Broadway show. You pay for your tickets and expect to be entertained. When you're not, you have a right to complain."

* "I can't believe they pay us for this - something we did for free as kids."

* "Don't call us heroes. Firemen are heroes."

* "The biggest mistake people make is when they bad-mouth people when they are fired. Once you bad-mouth people, you can't bring it back."

Denny McLain, *former pitcher: We were playing in Tiger Stadium and Mickey Mantle was coming up for one of the last times in his career. It was the ninth inning and we were ahead of the Yankees by something like 6-1. I called catcher Jim Price out to the mound and told him, "Listen, you or I will never get into the Hall of Fame, so why don't we do something to help somebody else?"*

He said: "What are you talking about?"

I said: "Let's see if Mantle can hit one out. He needs only one more home run to reach some kind of Yankee mark. So let's let him hit one."

Price said: "You've got to be kidding. That'd be cheating."

I said: "Oh, for God's sake, he can't hit a six-run homer"

Price asked what I wanted him to do. I told him: "When he gets into the batter's box, tell him to be ready."

When Mickey got in there, Price told him: "Be ready."

Mantle didn't know what he meant. Maybe he thought I was going to throw at him. I lobbed one up, about 65 miles and hour, and he took it for a strike.

Mantle looked at Price, then out at me.

Price said: "Listen, he's going to do that again - be ready!"

Mantle said: "Are you sure?"

Price said: "Yes, I am sure."

I lobbed another one and Mantle took it for strike two.

I knew Mickey was no brain surgeon but you don't take two pitches like that. Price came out again and said: "Now what do I do?"

I said: "Jim, just tell him to be ready."

The umpire knew what was going on but didn't say anything. Mantle fouled the next one off, then he put his hand out over the plate, belt high, telling me where he wanted it.

I threw squarely over the plate and he belted it into the upper deck in right. As he rounded third, he held up his hands and took his hat off. Mission accomplished.

Earl Wilson, *former pitcher: I made my first big league start in Tiger Stadium. It was this huge building with all green seats. Whenever I'd come through Detroit, I was impressed that black folks actually owned something. I grew up in the south and we didn't have much in those days. I walked along Boston Boulevard and saw all the fine homes and I'd say to myself: "I'd like to play here one day."*

That happened in 1966 and I guess the strange thing is I was the first player to have an agent - Bob Woolf of Boston. I'd had a pretty good year with the Tigers, winning 22 games, but was nervous about going in and asking for more money from general manager Jim Campbell.

Woolf told me not to worry. He'd stay back at the hotel and I could go to the phone and call him anytime I was having trouble with Campbell. I kept excusing myself, telling him I had to go to the bathroom, and I'd find a phone and call the hotel. I finally got what I wanted.

Years later, Campbell - a good guy - found out what I had done and he said, "I KNEW DAMN WELL YOU WEREN'T THAT SMART, WILSON!"

BEFORE THIS GUY KILLEBREW CAME ALONG WE WERE SAFE UP ON THIS LEFTFIELD ROOF.

CLANK

Harmon Killebrew, *former Minnesota Twins' third baseman: It's hard to believe I was the first one to hit a ball over the leftfield roof. I connected off Jim Bunning and why it went so far, I'll never know. The wind wasn't blowing.*

I saw the ball bounce once then disappear into the night. The funny thing is, the next day five fans tried to give me the ball.

Sparky Anderson was asked to pick his all-time Tiger team and, Sparky being Sparky, not only named the players but put them in his batting order:

1. Charlie Gehringer, second base: "A great line drive hitter - he'd be on base all day."

2. George Kell, third base: "He could shoot the ball into rightfield every time up, sending Gehringer to third. He could even do it while eating lunch."

3. Ty Cobb, centerfield: "The best hitter on the club, so I've got to put him where I get the most out of him."

4. Hank Greenberg, first base: "My lumber man. With this lineup, He could get 200 RBIs a season."

5. Harry Heilmann, leftfield: "A great-great hitter. He'd make them pitch to Greenberg."

6. Al Kaline, rightfield: "Al could spray the ball around and keep the rallies going."

7. Kirk Gibson, designated hitter: "He could power home Kaline and the runs would dance on the scoreboard."

8. Mickey Cochrane, catcher: "They always talk about his catching but he was a terrific hitter - maybe the fastest base runner of all the catchers in the history of the game."

9. Alan Trammell, shortstop: "He has to hit last in this lineup, but he is so consistent in everything he does, he would help us in every inning of every game."

Starting pitcher: Hal Newhouser. "I've never really had a great left-hander, and they tell me there were days when you couldn't touch him."

Reliever: "John Hiller or Willie Hernandez - I could go with either one."

Summary: *"I would be a certified genius managing these guys."*

When Ted Williams hit his game-winning homer with two-out in the ninth in the 1941 All-Star game, the photographers asked American League manager Del Baker of the Tigers if he'd give Williams a kiss.

"Heck," said Baker, "I'd kiss a porcupine if he could hit a home run like that for me."

When Tiger Stadium was known as Briggs Stadium, it was named after owner Walter O. Briggs, a multi-millionaire. He got his start at the age of 15 by working for the Michigan Central Railroad. He worked 14 to 16 hours a day and got paid $20 a month. But he got Sundays off.

Kirk Gibson didn't like talking to the press when he first joined the Tigers. He opened up as time went by. The writers began calling him "Kirk Glibson."

***George Kell**, former third baseman: I was a Tiger player for seven years and a broadcaster for another 38. That's 45 years and if I hadn't broken down like an old man is supposed to do (bad knee, bad back) I might still be broadcasting today. I loved it all.*

Hank Greenberg was the one who took me under his wing when I came to Detroit. I was having a good year, but one day I went 0-for-5 and the fans booed me. He came over to my locker after the game and said, "George, do you want me to tell you something? You've got it made." I looked at him and said, "What do you mean I've got it made?" He smiled. "They don't boo you in this town until you are successful."

One day the world champion roller skating king took in a game at Tiger Stadium and told Ty Cobb: "I'll give you a new pair of roller skates if you hit a home run for me."

Cobb went to the plate and pulled the second pitch over the rightfield fence. As he returned to the dugout, he stopped at the man's box and said: "What the hell would I do with a pair of roller skates!"

When third baseman Tom Brookens' wife had twins, he wondered if the Tigers would double his salary.

When ex-Tiger Richie Hebner retired from baseball, he resumed his career as a grave digger.

"Yeah," he said, "I'm working my way down in life."

Ex-outfielder Neil Chrisley asked: "When a player tests positive for drugs, why does it seem so negative?"

Bob Talbert, Free Press *columnist: I was blessed to come to Detroit in 1968 when the Tigers won the World Series. I was assigned to be, "Our Man in the Bleachers." It was wild. One day I wound up dictating my column from a phone booth in the back of the rightfield stands.*

We had season tickets, my wife and I, but before we got them, I liked to sit in all parts of the ball park because the people were so different. They were different in rightfield and different in leftfield, and we all know what it's like in the bleachers.

I enjoyed the kids the most. Not when they kicked the back of my seat. That wasn't any fun. I mean, when they showed up with their gloves and were convinced they would catch a foul ball before the game was over. I wish I could tell you how many kids thought they would grow up to be Alan Trammell ... that's what sitting in Tiger Stadium means to me.

Trainer Jack Homel asked: "How do you get a Dub-Dub in shape?" He said: "You rub a Dub-Dub."

From Jack Morris: "I always wondered - can arbitrators go to arbitration?"

Sparky Anderson didn't like umpire Doug Harvey's decision and went out to tell him about it.

Sparky said: "When I'm done, you're going to throw me out."

"You're out of here right now," said Harvey.

"I haven't said anything yet," said Sparky.

"That's right," said Harvey, "and you're not going to get the chance."

A sports writer covering the Tigers in spring training decided he would get a cake for his wife on her birthday and present it to her in their motel room.

When he lit all the candles, the fire alarm went off.

End of story.

Larry Parrish, *Tiger manager: I never felt comfortable at the plate in Tiger Stadium. I always thought home plate was turned a little bit to right-center. When I took my stance in the batter's box and I looked up, the pitcher wasn't where he was supposed to be. He was a little bit over my left shoulder.*

One night I knocked one into the rightfield seats. I think Jack Morris was the pitcher. After I went around the bases, Sparky Anderson came out and started arguing with the home plate umpire that the ball was foul. The home plate ump got the first base ump to change his mind, and darned if they didn't make me come out and hit again.

John Hiller, *former relief pitcher: The bullpen is a depressing place in Tiger Stadium. We had to invent things to make it interesting. We would play gin and one year Manager Mayo Smith put in a phone down there and we could make long distance calls all over the country and not pay for it.*

It was hard to watch the games through that steel screen. For a few years, we would bring high-powered field glasses out there with us and look at the girls in the left field seats. The catchers would bring portable home plates with them to warm us up and we'd get markers and hold them up for the ladies: "Meet us at the Lindell A.C." We'd hold the signs up and point to our backs so they could see our names. Sometimes it worked, sometimes it didn't. We did this before I was married. Of course.

Who's a hot head? In his first and only season as a player in the major leagues - with the Philadelphia Phillies in 1959 - Sparky Anderson was thrown out of the game 11 times.

Rookie Bill Freehan after practice in Tiger Stadium: "I don't want to get old. I don't even want to grow up."

When he was riding high, Denny McLain said he thought about running for president.

"I've even got my staff picked out," he said. "Joe Sparma will be my running mate because I've got to have the Italian vote, and Gates Brown will be my Secretary of Defense because I've got to get the black vote, too."

The airplane is shaking. The Tigers are caught in a violent storm. Pitcher Dan Petry gets up from his seat, goes down the aisle and sits next to Ernie Harwell, who is reading.

"Why'd you do that?" Petry is asked later.

He said: "Wherever Ernie was going, I wanted to go with him."

Our wonderful Overhang. Nobody else has one.

THAT OVERHANG

How did that rightfield overhang in Tiger Stadium come to be?

Simple. When the stands were double-decked after the 1937 season, Trumbull Avenue ran behind rightfield and there was no way to expand backward. So the upper deck was moved forward.

In mid-1959, the Tigers screened in the lower deck because home runs were too easy. When pitcher Paul Foytack was asked about it, he said: "That's great news. What about the upper deck?"

Reno Bertoia, *former infielder: Do I remember my first game at bat in the majors? Yes. It took place in Tiger Stadium. The pitcher threw me three pitches and I don't think I saw any of them. I was gone on strikes. His name? Satchel Paige. That was 1953.*

Al Kaline, former outfielder: The first time I saw Tiger Stadium was in 1953. It was called Briggs Stadium in those days. I saw it after a trip to St. Louis. We got off the train at about two in the morning. I was in a taxi with Johnny Pesky, the old pro from the Boston Red

Kaline's corner. Where's Al?

Sox. He was sort of my mentor, showing me the ropes. He said: "Al, look out the window. That's going to be your home in the future."

It looked like a big gray battleship. If you look at it from the side, it does look like a battleship. Or an aircraft carrier.

I was staying downtown at the Tuller Hotel and walked to the ball park the next day. I had a hard time getting in. I was only 18 years old and guards wouldn't believe I was one of the players.

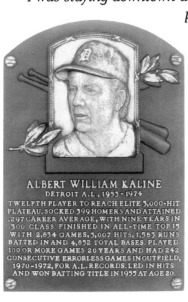

ALBERT WILLIAM KALINE
DETROIT A.L., 1953-1974
TWELFTH PLAYER TO REACH ELITE 3,000-HIT PLATEAU. SOCKED 399 HOMERS AND ATTAINED .297 CAREER AVERAGE, WITH NINE YEARS IN .300 CLASS. FINISHED IN ALL-TIME TOP 15 WITH 2,834 GAMES, 3,007 HITS, 1,583 RUNS BATTED IN AND 4,852 TOTAL BASES. PLAYED 100 OR MORE GAMES 20 YEARS AND HAD 242 CONSECUTIVE ERRORLESS GAMES IN OUTFIELD, 1970-1972, FOR A.L. RECORDS. LED IN HITS AND WON BATTING TITLE IN 1955 AT AGE 20.

The thing about playing rightfield in Tiger Stadium is that you're pretty close to the batter. It's also the sun field, and that makes it double tough. Your first step is the most important one because you can't hesitate on the play because the ball gets out there so quickly.

You always had to know where the wall was. It wasn't padded in those days.

Worst of Times, Best of Times

By Joe Falls

Gates Brown was retired. He was coaching the Tigers and I knew what a proud man he was. Very proud.

I thought I would have a little fun and one day I issued a challenge to him.

"Bet you 20 bucks you can't hit one out in five swings. You can pick any park in the league—even pick the pitcher."

He looked at me. He got a serious look. "You're on," he said, and thus began a sad and happy story.

I was only joshing with him but he took it seriously. He did take it as a challenge—a challenge of his manhood. While I kidded him in my paper about our bet, he began to take a lot of swings in batting practice.

He finally said; "Okay, I'm ready. I'm taking Seattle."

When the big night came, the whole team was stirred up about the bet. They were all pulling for Gates and some of the players wanted in on the action.

I covered all the bets and put something like $96 on home plate. Just to put a little extra pressure on my man.

Manager Sparky Anderson allowed us five minutes of batting practice to settle the issue.

I stood behind the batting cage as Gates stepped in to take his swings. He picked coach Dick Tracewski, a guy who could throw mush melons, as his pitcher.

Gates swung and the ball bounded down the first base line, foul.

I cried out: "One" I saw his face tighten up.

The next pitch hit the top of the batting cage. "Two!" I could see the veins starting to protrude from his neck.

What had I done? I could feel my face flush. I thought this would be fun but I saw now that I had put the man—this man I admired (hey, we had same birthdays)—in a terrible spot. The twenty bucks meant nothing.

He swung again, and again the ball hit the top of the cage. I didn't say anything. I could feel my face getting hotter.

Swing 4. Top of the cage. Dear God.

He had one swing left and swung with all his might—look at

Gates Brown: Our favorite pinch-hitter.

the picture–and the ball went screaming out to rightfield. It rose higher and higher and flew into the second deck, hitting a railing and skipping to the back of the stands.

The players let out a cheer and carried Gates off the field. I had this picture framed and gave it to Gates and it still hangs in his home in Detroit. I have one in my den, too.

Bill Freehan, *former catcher: I grew up around the 12 Mile-Woodward area and we'd either hitch a ride to the ball park or take a bus. We would sit in the bleachers and dream a little that maybe some day we might be down there playing for the Tigers. I never thought about what position I'd play. When you played on the sandlots, you didn't need a catcher. The screen was the catcher.*

I guess the biggest play I was ever involved in was when Willie Horton threw out Lou Brock in the 1968 World Series. We collided at the plate but neither of us fell down. Years later, Brock would say to me: "If I was out, why did you tag me again when I came back to the plate?" I said to him: "If you were safe, why did you come back to the plate?"

Jim Bunning, *former pitcher: Tiger Stadium was the first major league park I pitched in. The ball didn't carry then the way it does to-day, so I knew I could pitch to right-center and left-center. I kept the ball in hard and outside hard. But I did have to learn to pitch, and (chuckle) I didn't always get along with my manager (Charlie Dressen).*

I had this habit of falling on my left, landing on my glove or my hand, after I released the ball, and got a lot of criticism about it. They said I couldn't field balls hit to my right. But I got to balls on my left I normally couldn't reach. Anyway, we cheated with the third baseman. Because I was falling away from third base, we'd bring the third baseman in a few steps to cover that part of the field, and it worked. Only people who complained about me falling on my glove had trouble with this strategy.

INAUGURAL

They were not the Tigers yet but Detroit played its first game in the American League on April 25 1901. Milwaukee provided the opposition. Seats were arranged for 6,000 people but 10,023 showed up.

Baseball was very rudimentary. No white bases but sawdust filled gunny sacks which flew around when the players slid into them. The clubhouses were run-down shanties with no hot showers or even clean towels. The players dried themselves off with yesterday's towels.

Milwaukee took a 7-0 lead, which soon became 13-4. Amazingly, Detroit rallied for 10 runs in the bottom of the ninth to pull the game out 14-13.

It has never been that easy again.

Charlie Maxwell, *former outfielder: They always made a big deal out of me hitting home runs on Sunday. I could never understand why I did it, but I guess I did it a lot.*

It started on May 3, 1959. We'd just changed managers. They let Bill Norman go because we got off to such a terrible start and brought in Jimmy Dykes from Pittsburgh.

I hit four homers in a row in the doubleheader - my last time up in the first game, then three in a row to start the second game. Van Patrick, who was broadcasting the games, made a big deal of it, but I could never explain how it all happened.

Max Lapides was a true fan of the Tigers. Even though he was due to work, he had to see the final game of the 1968 World Series, so instead of going to the office, he hopped a plane to St. Louis the morning of the game.

After the Tigers won, he got on another plane back to Detroit and the party was on. Tiger fans like himself were having a wild time and who cared if the pilot told them they couldn't land at Metro Airport because it was overrun by people waiting for the team to come home.

They were detoured to Dayton. Dayton-Schmaton. The Tigers were champions of the world and they all went into the airport lounge, hung up their signs and banners and the celebration went on.

Max noticed some guy sitting at the far end of the bar and he looked as if he had lost his last friend.

He went up to him said: "How are you, my friend? Is there anything wrong?"

"It's all you loonies," he said. "I got on the plane in Oklahoma City and then I run into you in St. Louis and now I'm sitting in a bar in Dayton, Ohio. Nothing wrong with that except I am supposed to be in Detroit because I was to get married tonight."

Billy Rogell, *former player from the 1930s: Back in those days, the clubhouses were right across the way from each other on the third base side of the field. You had to go through our dugout to get to first base. For some reason, Babe Ruth used to come out early and sit on our bench and talk with all our guys. I never met a nicer man in all my life. He was the only guy that people would get up and scream, "THERE'S THE BABE!" as he walked across the field.*

He called me "The Little Guy." One day I knocked one into the street in left and it bounced into a passing truck. They never found it again. When Ruth got to second base, I said: "How'd you like that one, Babe?" He laughed.

Bits and . . .

The only player who wasn't afraid of Ty Cobb? Cobb said it was the Old Dutchman, shortstop Honus Wagner of the Pittsburgh Pirates.

"As hard as I tried, I couldn't scare him," said Cobb.

What Detroit slugger stuck out Ted Williams in his only appearance as a pitcher in the major leagues?

It was Rudy York, the Indian first baseman, on Aug. 24, 1940.

Here's one: What Tiger player was born in a city whose name was the same as his?

It was Slim Love of Love, Missouri.

DR. STANLEY, I PRESUME!

SS

CF

1968

Mickey Stanley, former outfielder: I would like to say one thing about playing shortstop in the 1968 World Series. I didn't enjoy the Series at all. Not one bit. I was scared stiff all the time because I didn't want to let the guys down.

I had no idea this was going to happen. I liked to take ground balls at shortstop before the games. It was my way of loosening up, getting rid of the tension. Mayo Smith, our manager, saw me do it and called me to his room in Baltimore about eight days before the end of the season. He wanted to get Al Kaline back in the lineup. Al was hurt. He could do it this way, and he told me I could do the job. Norm Cash kept telling me the same thing, but I wasn't so sure. Would I know how to make all the plays? I saw them from the outfield but now I was seeing them from the other end.

Lou Brock, the first batter, intentionally hit a grounder to me with that inside-out swing of his. When I picked it up, I thought, "Well, if you're going to throw it away, throw it hard. Don't lollipop it over there." I gunned it and we got him, but none of it was enjoyable.

Can you name the Tiger player who is buried in Arlington Cemetery?

Lu Blue, first baseman from the 1920s.

The only Tiger pitcher ever to win a Gold Glove award was . . . Frank Lary.

When pitcher Lou Kretlow finished pitching for the Tigers in 1949, he became a golf pro and was credited with a 427-yard hole-in-one.

"Heck," he said, "I used to throw 'em further than that in my pitching days."

Mark Fidrych, who never had an agent: "Why should I give anyone 10 percent when I do all the work?"

Ty Cobb was the first player to have a candy bar named after him.

Ferris Fain, who played first base for the Tigers in 1955, had a father who was a jockey and finished second in the 1912 Kentucky Derby.

***Sparky Anderson**, former manager: I loved managing in Detroit. I could hide in the dugout, so the other team couldn't see me. I'd use the posts to hide behind. I'd work the middle post, then switch to the right post, then to the left post. They could never see me from across the way. The third base coach could look in at me but he could see only the top half of my body. So, I'd work the steps. Right foot on the step, that was a bunt. Left foot, a steal. I could put both feet on the steps and lean on the post and that was the hit-and-run.*

And the best thing of all, I was so small I never hit my head on the dugout roof like so many of the other guys did. I wonder if they'd let me have the posts in the dugout when they take the place down. I could hide from my wife and go play golf.

Which Tiger pitcher had a daughter in the LPGA Hall of Fame?

George Suggs (1908-09), father of golfing great Louise Suggs.

Ty Cobb was the first player to come to the plate swinging three bats at the same time.

Mathematicians figured out that Hank Greenberg would have hit 581 home runs instead of 331 if he had not lost nearly five years in the Army during World War II.

Centerfielder Don Demeter went 266 games in a row without making an error. The streak came to an end when a dog ran on the field and distracted him in making a throw after he cleanly fielded the ball.

TRY TO OUTFOX ME, WILL THEY?

Jim Northrup, *former outfielder: When I was a kid, my father used to take me to Tiger Stadium to see Ted Williams play. We'd go down once a year and it was about a five-hour drive from our home in St. Louis, Michigan, since there were no expressways in those days.*

So, here I was, a kid off the farm who never saw anything bigger than a silo and I'm sitting in this marvelous green stadium - the biggest building I ever saw.

Later on, when I played for the Tigers, I realized it would have been better if I had played in another place. It was 440 to centerfield and I was a straightaway hitter. It must have cost me 10 home runs a year - just like the deep rightfield in Fenway Park cost Carl Yastrzemski his share of homers.

But it was in Tiger Stadium where we won it all and I'll never forget throwing our owner, John Fetzer, into the whirlpool the night we clinched the pennant. He loved it.

Dan Petry, *former pitcher: I re-member the night games the best. The stadium was quiet. Ev-eryone had gone home. Instead of walking through the con-course to my car, I would go back down through the tunnel to the dug-out. I'd walk directly across the field. I'd look around the darkened stadium, at all the empty seats. I'd be thinking, "Here's a 20- or 21-year-old kid from California, the land of sunshine and palm trees, and I'm in the middle of Michigan, and it feels great." Before I joined the Tigers, I couldn't have found Michigan on a map, but now this was my home and I loved it. I still love it, which is why I've made my home here.*

Dan Ewald, *former baseball writer and publicity director of the team: When you're born into Detroit, you're a born Tiger fan. It's almost like being given a name. I was born right down the street from the ballpark. My mom and grandparents raised me after my father died. My grand-father was a blue-collar worker but he always had enough money to take me to the games on Sunday afternoons.*

We'd get there early and I'd try to catch foul balls. I could see the amused look on his face but he let me do it. I got five of them, which wasn't much, but it was five more than most kids got.

We lived right off Michigan Avenue, about a mile away, and it was an easy walk to the ball park. In those days, everybody walked. They had a trolley which ran down Michigan Avenue but it was more fun to stroll and look at all the sights. I'd sneak in and the way you did it was look for a family of five or six and kind of nudge in line ahead of them. The ticket taker would wave you through, thinking that Dad at the end of the line would have your ticket. He couldn't keep track of everyone, but it didn't matter. The minute I got in, I'd race up the ramp and hide.

We had to walk past all the meat packing places on Michigan Av-enue and that was always an experience. The odors would just over-power you. But we didn't mind. It was part of going to the ball park. It meant you were getting close.

Ty Cobb was named manager of the Tigers in 1921. He immediately told the players how to prepare for retirement.

"Buy a few shares of Coca-Cola," Cobb told them. It was selling for $1.18 a share. "And after you buy it, don't sell it for a little profit. Forget about it for a few years." Eight years later the stock sold for $181 a share and that's how Cobb became a millionaire."

A weird one was Bill Coughlin, who played first base from 1905 through 1908. He was known as "Rowdy Bill." He spit tobacco juice all over Bennett Park and accidentally shot off the first finger on his left hand.

Stat: Charlie Maxwell hit 40 of his 148 career home runs on a Sunday.

Irwin Cohen, *former front office employee and baseball historian: After the 1984 season, the Tigers went to a computerized ticket system. Against a schematic of every section, I had to physically count every seat and bleacher space in the ball park.*

I found seven seats the ticket office never knew about - six in the top rows of the upper deck down the rightfield line and a box seat in the visitors bullpen area. The ushers knew about these seats but the ticket department didn't. Tickets were never printed for them.

I saw my first game when I was 8-years-old and had no idea what the ball park would look like. This was in 1950 - the days before we had television. I thought it would be like the playgrounds, with no grass in the infield. I was shocked to see the grass. I had always listened to the games on the radio and I expected to hear Harry Heilmann broadcasting the game in the stands.

When I worked for the Tigers, I had Frank Navin's old desk and big round-backed chair. It reeked of history. It was probably from when Navin Field opened in 1912 as there were pictures of Ty Cobb signing his contract on the desk while the owner, Navin is leaning back in his chair beaming.

Stat: Denny McLain and Dizzy Dean wore the same No. 17 when they won 30 games pitching for their pennant-winning teams.

Detroit was the first major league team to issue rain checks. It happened in 1890 and each ticket read: "In case rain interrupts the game on this date before three innings are played, this rain check will admit bearer to grounds for next league game only."

Bobo Newsom won 20 games for the Tigers in 1940. He was so pleased he bought a car with the loudest horn the factory could turn out and it played, "Hold That Tiger!" He even reserved a table at a leading downtown restaurant for the entire next season so he could entertain friends. Then he went out and lost 20 games.

Brothers Jerry and Hub Walker broke in with the Tigers in 1931. The Yankees made them bigger offers but their mother wouldn't let her two Southern sons sign with any team named "Yankees."

Ralph Snyder, *former stadium manager: The World Series of 1984 was memorable because of all the crazy things that happened around the ball park on that final Sunday game.*

Vice president George Bush was there and there were secret service agents all over the place. They set up their own short wave radio station and put snipers in the light towers. Peter Ueberroth, who was the commissioner of baseball, had his limousine trashed when he left after the game was over.

The writers couldn't leave because there were too many disturbances in the street, so Tom Monaghan, our owner, had his people land his helicopter in the middle of the stadium and bring pizzas to those working in the press box.

John McHale, Sr., played football and baseball at Briggs Stadium. He played for Catholic Central in the annual Goodfellow football game in 1939, then played first base for the Tigers starting in 1943.

George (Tweedy) Stallings, the Tigers' first manager at Bennett Park in 1896, studied medicine at the College of Physicians and Surgeons in Baltimore and believed losing streaks were caused by loose pieces of paper floating in front of the player's bench. He ordered groundskeepers to pick up any loose paper before the games.

When Claude Agee signed a minor league contract in August, 1953, the Tigers became the last major league team to sign a black player to their organization.

They said it:

Mickey Lolich: "The only thing running and exercising can do for you is make you happy."

Bill Scherer: "I never had a pet rock because they have to die some day and I don't like to see anything die."

Fred Smith, *baseball historian: The ball park was different in the 1920s. When the Philadelphia A's came to town, I'd sit in the leftfield pavilion and wait for Al Simmons to come up. He could really put them over the wall. When he'd hit one, we'd run to the far end of the pavilion and watch the ball bounce in the street. If Simmons didn't do it, Jimmie Foxx did.*

One day I saw Ty Cobb score from second on an infield out. He caught them all by surprise. After the game, the kids waited for him to come out. I was in front of the pack and Cobb put his arm around me and spoke to me. He told me to stay in school, study hard and be a good kid.

He lived on the corner of Burlingame and Second. I lived three blocks away and I'd go over there and stare at his house. But I never saw him there.

How did Michigan and Trumbull get their names?

William Woodbridge bought the acerage that would include the site of Tiger Stadium in 1819. It was called Michigan Grand Avenue. In 1837, it was changed to Michigan Ave.

Woodbridge became a state senator, governor and U.S. Senator and named a dirt road running through the property Trumbull, after his father-in-law poet, John Trumbull.

The broadcast booth in Tiger Stadium is closer to the field than any booth in the major leagues. Announcer Jon Miller said: "One day I was doing a broadcast for the Oakland A's and Gene Tenace got hit by a foul ball. He fell to the ground writhing in pain and I said, 'That must really hurt." Tenace looked up at the booth and said: 'It sure does.'"

***Alan Trammell**, former shortstop: Lou Whitaker and I were called up at the same time. We got a cab in from the airport and the driver said: "Hey, guys, that's Tiger Stadium right ahead of us." I looked out the window and my first thought was that it looked like a warehouse.*

What got me was all the seats were made of wood. I'd watch the balls go crashing into the upper deck in batting practice and the wood would be flying all over the place. What a great place to play ball.

***Frank Tanana**, former pitcher. . . I pitched in Tiger Stadium when I was a kid but the day that will stay with me forever was the day I pitched near the end of my career. It was the final game of the 1987 season against Toronto–the day we completed our comeback and clinched the division with a 1-0 victory.*

We battled the Blue Jays all year. If we win, we finish first. If we lose, then it's playoff. Jimmie Key started for Toronto and pitched a great game. Sparky Anderson gave me the ball and Larry Herndon hit a home run and I made it stand up with a complete game. How could anyone forget such a day?

Steve Boros, *former third baseman: My father owned a grocery store in Flint and the greatest day of the year was the one Sunday when he got the whole family together and take us to Tiger Stadium for a ball game. What I remember is listening to Harry Heilmann broadcast the games on the radio. He would scare me half to death. When the other team would smack one, he'd say: "It's trouble, it's trouble." That meant it was going for extra bases. I held my breath and hoped he wouldn't say "double trouble" because that meant it was in the seats.*

Mickey Lolich, *former pitcher: How can I ever forget the fifth game of the 1968 World Series? We were trailing three games to one and had to have the game to stay alive.*

The thing is, I forgot about the pre-game ceremonies, and so did my pitching coach, Johnny Sain.

I had a special routine about warming up. I would go down to the bullpen about 15 minutes before the game and I would throw "x" amount of warm-up pitches. That usually took about 12 minutes.

I started warming up. You have to remember that at this time of the year the bullpen is in the shadows at game time. I got halfway through my routine and all of a sudden they're doing the national anthem. Jose Feliciano is singing it and it lasts forever. No one is sure what he is singing but he goes on and on.

I started cooling down. The umpire comes out and says: "Come on, Mick. We gotta get the game started." He told me the game was on national television.

So, I go the mound and all I can throw right away are fast balls and Orlando Cepeda smacks a three-run homer into the leftfield seats. Luckily, I was able to settle down and we won the game. I even got a hit to keep a rally going.

BOO BIRDS

The charm of Tiger Stadium is that many of the fans are close to the field. Sometimes, too close.

"I liked to listen to them," said George Kell, who was very close to them at third base. "One day, Hal Newhouser was getting rocked by the Boston Red Sox and one fan was all over him. I could hear every word he said, so I went over to Hal to calm him down.

"I said, 'Hang in there, Hal. Don't let that guy get to you.' And then I heard the fan say, 'And you're not doing so good yourself, Kell.'"

Mike Ilitch, owner: *I was very lucky as a kid because I shagged fly balls for Hank Greenberg on the morning of the games. Two Tiger scouts arranged for me to get out of school and go to the ballpark a couple of days a week. I was dumbfounded when Greenberg stepped into the batting cage and couldn't get the ball out of the infield. I'd be waiting in the outfield but the ball could barely reach the outfield grass.*

I knew the balls looked dark and when I picked one up, it was wet. It was water logged. It was very heavy.

It turned out that Hank used three sets of balls–the water-logged ones, the slightly older balls and then some brand new ones. What a smart man. It was like swinging a heavier bat before stepping in to hit.

When he got to the new balls, they'd go flying into the upper deck and I'd say to myself: "THAT is the Hank Greenberg I've been watching since I was a little baby."

Jim Hendricks, *radio and TV sportscaster: Tiger Stadium was a legend. I can remember turning in 2-cent bottles and paper drives just to get 60 cents for a bleacher seat. My mother would pack a lunch and I'd go down to the ball park by 11 in the morning. The game didn't start until three and I was hungry by game time.*

I got a job in the commissary and I was a "bun runner." A "bun runner" was someone whom they said to, "We need 14 dozen buns at Concession Stand No. 14 in leftfield." You'd go down to the commissary and load up a cart and push it up those ramps. THAT was a "bun runner" . . . buns, canisters of pop or hot dogs, whatever they needed.

I worked in the clubhouse and saw all the players up close–Joe DiMaggio, what a gentleman. Casey Stengel used to swipe my cheese sandwiches and he'd give me a dollar to get some hot dogs.

I went to Catholic school and got the job only because the Sister allowed me to skip 16 afternoons and that's when we had religion. It was the closest I ever came to kissing a nun.

Paul W. Smith, *WJR personality: My memory is probably different from all those who played at Tiger Stadium, or broadcast the games. My big moment didn't come in the 50s, 60s, 70s or 80s. It was the 90s when I felt a true rush of history. That's when I worked from the field myself and could feel Ty Cobb, Hank Greenberg, Al Kaline and all the other greats around me. And it was standing there, near home plate, that I met for the first time the likes of Sonny Eliot, Pete Waldmeir, Bob Talbert and other people in our profession. I could not get over the fact I was standing in a place I never could have gotten to as an athlete.*

Lance Parrish, *former catcher: There is no ballpark quite like Tiger Stadium . . . the atmosphere, the electricity–you can't get that feeling in any other park. The people are so close to you that you can almost touch them. You certainly can see them and hear them.*

I recall the first time I saw somebody hit a ball out of the park. Jason Thompson put one over the roof in right. I grew up with him and always knew how far he could hit a ball. But to see it sail over the roof . . . it was majestic.

Farewell, my lovely.

Cast of Characters

Joe Falls, who never got a base hit in his life, works for The Detroit News and will tell you what's wrong or right with the Tigers and you don't even have to ask him. Right, Joe baby?

Irwin Cohen, sometimes known as Mr. Baseball, was editor and publisher of the Baseball Bulletin and worked in the front office of the Tigers. He is the only man ever to count every seat in Tiger Stadium. A nice job, but he missed the rest rooms.

Doc Holcomb, formerly of The Detroit News, did not take pictures of Abraham Lincoln. It just seems that way. He has been at his profession for 60 years and has learned not to put his index finger over the lens.

Dick Mayer, who is semi-retired as an artist for the Detroit Free Press, thinks he is Rod Laver, the great tennis player. It turns out his pen is mightier than his racquet.

Connie Sweet is as sweet as her name. She is president, vice president, secretary and treasurer of her own company and managed to design this book in spite of working with all these guys. It's amazing that her name didn't change to Connie Sour.

ECH◉ES of TIGER STADIUM

Available in a double cassette and a three compact disc edition.

Cassette

CD

3 hours of recordings include interviews and memoirs of:

George Cantor	Larry Parrish	Fred Smith
Kirk Gibson	Mark Fidrych	Billy Rogell
Fr. Vincent Horken	Dave Bergman	Alan Trammell
Willie Horton	Max Lapides	Bill Freehan
Jim Schmakel	Sonny Eliot	Mike Ilitch
Jim Price	George Kell	Mickey Lolich
Ted Williams	John Hiller	Sparky Anderson
Paul Carey	Mickey Stanley	Jim Northrup
Virgil Trucks	Bob Talbert	Irwin Cohen
Jack Morris	Earl Wilson	Dan Petry
Frank Fenick	Denny McLain	Dan Ewald
Frank Beckmann	Harmon Killebrew	Jim Hendricks
Mayor Dennis Archer	Ernie Harwell	Lance Parrish
Tom Gage	Charlie Maxwell	Frank Tanana
Tony Clark	Ralph Snyder	Jim Bunning
John McHale, Jr.	Al Kaline	Paul W. Smith
Gates Brown	Steve Boros	

NAME ———————————————————————

ADDRESS ————————————————————— APT. NO. ———

CITY ——————————————————— STATE ——— ZIP —————

Mail to:
Echoes of Tiger Stadium
17117 W. 9 Mile Rd.
Suite. 1725
Southfield, MI 48075

Or charge by calling:
1-877-OLD PARK
1-877 653-7275

Please allow four weeks for delivery.

$14.95 Cassettes	Qty.	—————
$19.95 CDs	Qty	—————

❑ Check
❑ VISA #:———————————————
  Exp. Date:———————————
❑ MC #:———————————————
  Exp. Date:———————————

Sub Total:	$	—————
Shipping/Handling:		$6.00
Total:	$	—————

S&H charges apply only to first product order, additional quantities shipped at no charge.